1,000,000 Books

are available to read at

www.ForgottenBooks.com

Read online
Download PDF
Purchase in print

ISBN 978-0-282-42108-3
PIBN 10851231

This book is a reproduction of an important historical work. Forgotten Books uses state-of-the-art technology to digitally reconstruct the work, preserving the original format whilst repairing imperfections present in the aged copy. In rare cases, an imperfection in the original, such as a blemish or missing page, may be replicated in our edition. We do, however, repair the vast majority of imperfections successfully; any imperfections that remain are intentionally left to preserve the state of such historical works.

Forgotten Books is a registered trademark of FB &c Ltd.
Copyright © 2018 FB &c Ltd.
FB &c Ltd, Dalton House, 60 Windsor Avenue, London, SW19 2RR.
Company number 08720141. Registered in England and Wales.

For support please visit www.forgottenbooks.com

1 MONTH OF FREE READING

at
www.ForgottenBooks.com

By purchasing this book you are eligible for one month membership to ForgottenBooks.com, giving you unlimited access to our entire collection of over 1,000,000 titles via our web site and mobile apps.

To claim your free month visit:
www.forgottenbooks.com/free851231

* Offer is valid for 45 days from date of purchase. Terms and conditions apply.

English
Français
Deutsche
Italiano
Español
Português

www.forgottenbooks.com

Mythology Photography **Fiction** Fishing Christianity **Art** Cooking Essays Buddhism Freemasonry Medicine **Biology** Music **Ancient Egypt** Evolution Carpentry Physics Dance Geology **Mathematics** Fitness Shakespeare **Folklore** Yoga Marketing **Confidence** Immortality Biographies Poetry **Psychology** Witchcraft Electronics Chemistry History **Law** Accounting **Philosophy** Anthropology Alchemy Drama Quantum Mechanics Atheism Sexual Health **Ancient History Entrepreneurship** Languages Sport Paleontology Needlework Islam **Metaphysics** Investment Archaeology Parenting Statistics Criminology **Motivational**

MAN VISIBLE AND INVISIBLE

EXAMPLES OF DIFFERENT TYPES OF MEN AS
SEEN BY MEANS OF TRAINED CLAIRVOYANCE

BY
C. W. LEADBEATER

WITH
FRONTISPIECE, THREE DIAGRAMS, AND TWENTY-TWO
COLOURED ILLUSTRATIONS

NEW YORK
JOHN LANE: THE BODLEY HEAD
1903

BP565
.L52
1903

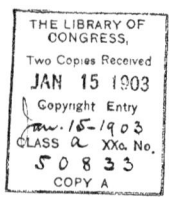

COPYRIGHT
BY
JOHN LANE
1903

FIRST EDITION PUBLISHED JANUARY, 1903

PRINTED BY THE PUBLISHERS PRINTING CO.
NEW YORK, U. S. A.

AUTHOR'S NOTE·

THE Author wishes to express his very hearty acknowledgments to two Theosophical colleagues who have prepared for him the illustrations of this book—to Count Maurice Prozor, who drew and coloured them for him from the life, and to Miss Gertrude Spink, who spent many days in patiently copying them with the air-brush, in order that they might be more successfully reproduced by the photographic process.

CONTENTS

CHAPTER		PAGE
I	How these Things are Known	1
II	The Planes of Nature	7
III	Clairvoyant Sight	13
IV	Man's Vehicles	20
V	The Trinity	26
VI	The Earlier Outpourings	36
VII	The Animal Group-Soul	42
VIII	The Upward Curve	46
IX	Human Consciousness	52
X	The Third Outpouring	59
XI	How Man Evolves	70
XII	What His Bodies Show Us	76
XIII	What the Colours Mean	80
XIV	The Savage	87
XV	The Ordinary Person	92
XVI	Sudden Emotions	96
XVII	More Permanent Conditions	104
XVIII	The Developed Man	117
XIX	The Health-Aura	128
XX	The Causal Body of the Adept	135

LIST OF ILLUSTRATIONS

PLATE			
I	Signification of the Colours	*Frontispiece*	
II	The Planes of Nature	*page*	20
III	The Three Outpourings	"	38
IV	Involution and Evolution	"	46
V	The Causal Body of the Savage		66
VI	The Mental Body of the Savage		87
VII	The Astral Body of the Savage		88
VIII	The Causal Body of the Average Man	"	91
IX	The Mental Body of the Average Man	"	93
X	The Astral Body of the Average Man	"	94
XI	A Sudden Rush of Affection	"	96
XII	A Sudden Rush of Devotion	"	98
XIII	Intense Anger	"	100
XIV	A Shock of Fear	"	103
XV	The Average Man in Love	"	107
XVI	The Irritable Man	"	109
XVII	The Miser	"	110
XVIII	Deep Depression	"	112
XIX	The Devotional Type	"	114
XX	The Scientific Type	"	116
XXI	The Causal Body of the Developed Man	"	118
XXII	The Mental Body of the Developed Man	"	121
XXIII	The Astral Body of the Developed Man	"	123
XXIV	The Normal Health-Aura	"	128
XXV	The Health-Aura in Disease	"	132
XXVI	The Causal Body of the Arhat	"	138

MAN VISIBLE AND INVISIBLE

Chapter I

HOW THESE THINGS ARE KNOWN

Man is a curiously complex being, and his evolution, past, present and future, is a study of perennial interest for all who can see and understand. Through what toilsome eternities of gradual development he has come to be what he is, to what round in the long ladder of his progress he has now attained, what possibilities of further progress the veil of the future conceals from us, these are questions to which few can be indifferent—questions which have been occurring all through the ages to every one who has thought at all.

Among us in the Western world the answers given have been many and various. There has been much dogmatic assertion, based on differing interpretations of alleged revelation; there have been many ingenious speculations, the fruit in some cases of close metaphysical reasoning. But dogmatism meets us with a story which is on the face of it manifestly impossible, while speculation moves chiefly along entirely materialistic lines, and endeavours to arrive at a satisfactory result by ignoring half of the phenomena for which we have to account. Neither dogmatism nor speculation approaches the problem from a practical point of view, as a matter which can be studied and investigated like any other science.

Theosophy comes forward with a theory based upon entirely different foundations. While in no way depreciating the knowledge to be gained either by study of the ancient scriptures or by philosophical reasoning, it nevertheless regards the constitution and the evolution of man as matters, not of speculation, but of simple investigation—not of vague theory, but of definite fact. Its statement is perfectly clear; the past, the present, and the future of man may be examined at first-hand by all who will take the trouble to qualify themselves for the study. When so examined, they prove to be parts of a magnificent scheme, coherent and readily comprehensible—a scheme which, while it agrees with and explains much of the old religious teaching, is yet in no way dependent on it, since it can be verified at every step by the use of the inner faculties which, though as yet latent in the majority of mankind, have already been brought into working order by a considerable number among our students.

For the past history of man, this theory depends not only upon the concurrent testimony of the tradition of the earlier religions, but upon the examination of a definite record—a record which can be seen and consulted by any one who possesses the degree of clairvoyance requisite to appreciate the vibrations of the finely-subdivided matter upon which it is impressed. For its knowledge as to the future which awaits humanity, it depends, first, upon logical deduction from the character of the progress already made; secondly, on direct information supplied by men who have already reached those conditions which for most of us still constitute a more or less remote future; and thirdly, on the comparison which any one who has the privilege of seeing them may make between highly-evolved men at various levels. We can imagine that a child who did not otherwise know the course of nature might reason that he would presently grow up and become a man, merely from the fact that he had already grown to a certain extent and in a certain way, and that he saw around him other children and young people at every stage of growth between his own and the adult level.

The study of the condition of man at the

present time, of the immediate methods for his evolution, and of the effect upon that evolution of his thoughts, his emotions, his actions—all this is regarded by Theosophical students as a mere matter of the application of well-known laws as a broad, general principle, and then of careful observation, of painstaking comparison of many cases in order to comprehend the detailed working of these laws. It is, in fact, simply a question of sight, and this book is published in the hope, first, that it may help earnest students who do not yet possess this sight to realise how the soul and its vehicles really appear when examined by its means; and secondly, that the very large number of persons who are now beginning to exercise this vision more or less perfectly, may by it be helped to understand the *meaning* of what they see.

I am perfectly aware that the world at large is not yet convinced of the very existence of this power of clairvoyant sight; but I also know that all who have really studied the question have found the evidence for it irresistible, and we can afford to ignore the very positive convictions which are usually so vehemently expressed by those who have *not* studied it. I will venture to say that if any intelligent person will take the trouble to read the stories—the authenticated stories—quoted in my little book on *Clair-*

voyance, and will then turn from them to the books from which they were selected, he will see at once that there is an overwhelming mass of irrefutable evidence in favour of the existence of this faculty. To those who themselves can see, and are daily in the habit of exercising this higher vision in a hundred different ways, the denial of the ignorant majority that such sight is possible naturally seems ridiculous. For the clairvoyant the question is not worth arguing. If a blind man came up to us and assured us that there was no such thing as ordinary physical sight, and that we were deluded in supposing that we possessed this faculty, we in our turn should probably not feel it worth while to argue at great length in defence of our supposed delusion. We should simply say: "I certainly do see, and it is useless to try to persuade me that I do not; all the daily experiences of my life show me that I do; I decline to be argued out of my definite knowledge of positive facts." Now this is precisely how the trained clairvoyant feels when ignorant people serenely pronounce that it is quite impossible that he should possess a power which he is at that very moment using to read the thoughts of the wiseacres who deny it to him!

I am not attempting, therefore, in this book to prove that clairvoyance is a reality; I take that for granted, and proceed to describe what is seen by its means. Neither will I here repeat the details given in the little book which I have mentioned as to the methods of clairvoyance, but will confine myself to such brief statement of the broad principles of the subject as is absolutely necessary in order that this book shall be comprehensible to one who has not studied other Theosophical literature.

CHAPTER II

THE PLANES OF NATURE

IN order to enunciate even these broad principles, however, it is necessary to begin by explaining some of the facts discovered by the use of this very faculty. The first point which must be clearly comprehended is the wonderful complexity of the world around us—the fact that it includes enormously more than comes within the range of ordinary vision.

We are all aware that matter exists in different conditions, and that it may be made to change its conditions by variation of pressure and temperature. We have the three well known states of matter, the solid, the liquid and the gaseous, and it is the theory of science that all substances can, under proper variation of temperature and pressure, exist in all these conditions. There are still, I think, a few substances which chemists have not succeeded in reducing from one state to another; but it is universally believed that just as water may become ice at a lower temperature, and steam at a higher one, so every solid which we know might become liquid or gaseous under proper conditions; every liquid may be made solid or gaseous, every gas may be liquefied and even solidified. We know that air itself has been liquefied, and that some of the other gases have been reduced to a solid slab.

Occult chemistry shows us another and higher condition than the gaseous, into which also all substances known to us can be translated or transmuted; and to that condition we have given the name of etheric. That which science postulates as ether is found by occult chemistry to be not a homogeneous body, but simply another state of matter; not itself a new kind of substance, but ordinary matter reduced to a particular state. We may have, for example, hydrogen in an etheric condition instead of as a gas; we may have gold or silver or any other element either as a solid, a liquid or a gas, or in this other higher state which we call etheric. Just as we find in the world about us some elements normally solid, as is gold; some normally liquid, as is mercury; and some normally gaseous, as is oxygen, so there are substances which are normally etheric—which ordinarily exist in that condition, though by special treatment they can be brought down to the gaseous condition, or raised to some other state still finer than their own.

In ordinary science we speak of an atom of oxygen, an atom of hydrogen, an atom of any of the sixty or seventy substances which chemists call elements, the theory being that that is an element which cannot be further reduced, and that each of these elements has its atom—and an atom, as we may see from the Greek derivation of the word, means that which cannot be cut, or further subdivided. Occult science tells us, what many scientists have frequently suspected, that all these so-called elements are not in the true sense of the word elements at all; that what we call an atom of oxygen or hydrogen is not the ultimate, and in fact is not an atom at all, but a molecule which can under certain circumstances be broken up into atoms. By repeating this breaking-up process it is found that we arrive eventually at an infinite number of definite physical atoms which are all alike; so that there is one substance at the back of all substances, and different combinations of its ultimate atoms give us what in chemistry are called atoms of oxygen or hydrogen, gold or silver, lithium or platinum, etc. When these are all broken up we get back to a set of atoms which are all identical, except that some of them are positive and some negative.

The study of these atoms and of the possibilities of their combination is in itself one of most enthralling interest, though foreign to our present subject; but those specially interested in the matter may be referred to Mrs. Besant's article upon Occult Chemistry in *Lucifer* for November 1895. Even these, however, are found to be atoms only from the point of view of our physical plane; that is to say, there are methods by which even they can be subdivided, but when they are so broken up they give us matter belonging to a different realm of nature—matter which is not expansible by any degree of heat which we are able to produce, or contractible by any degree of cold with which we are acquainted. Yet this higher matter also is not simple but complex; and we find that it also exists in a series of states of its own, corresponding very fairly to the states of physical matter which we call solid, liquid, gaseous or etheric. Again, by carrying on our process of subdivision far enough we reach another atom—the atom of that realm of nature to which occultists have given the name of the astral world.

Then the whole process may be repeated; for by further subdivision of that astral atom we find ourselves dealing with another still higher and more refined world, though a world which is still material. Once again we find matter existing in definitely marked conditions corresponding at that much higher level to the states with which we are familiar; and the ultimate result of our investigations brings us once again to an atom—the atom of this third great realm of nature, which in Theosophy we call the mental world. So far as we know, there is no limit to this possibility of subdivision, but there is a very distinct limit to our capability of observing it. However, we can see enough to be certain of the existence of a considerable number of these different realms, each of which is in one sense a world in itself, though in another and wider sense all are parts of one stupendous whole.

In our literature these different realms of nature are frequently spoken of as planes, because in our study it is sometimes convenient to image them as one above another, according to the different degrees of density of the matter of which they are composed. It will be seen that in the accompanying diagram (Plate II.) they are drawn in this way; but it must be very carefully borne in mind that this arrangement is merely adopted for convenience and as a symbol, and that it in no way represents the actual relations of these various planes. They must not be imagined as lying above one another like the shelves of a book-case, but rather as filling the same space and interpenetrating one another. It is a fact well known to science that even in the hardest substances no two atoms ever touch one another; always each atom has its field of action and vibration, and every molecule in turn has its larger field; so that there is always space between them under any possible circumstances. Every physical atom is floating in an astral sea—a sea of astral matter which surrounds it and fills every interstice in this physical matter. It is universally recognised that ether interpenetrates all known substances, the densest solid as well as the most rarefied gas; and just as it moves with perfect freedom between the particles of the denser matter, so does astral matter interpenetrate it in turn, and move with perfect freedom among its particles. The mental matter in its turn interpenetrates the astral in precisely the same manner; so that all these different realms of nature are not in any way separated in space, but are all existing around us and about us here and now, so that to see them and to investigate them it is not necessary for us to make any movement in space, but only to open within ourselves the senses by means of which they can be perceived.

CHAPTER III

CLAIRVOYANT SIGHT

THIS brings before us another very important consideration. All these varieties of finer matter exist not only in the world without, but they exist in man also. He has not only the physical body which we see, but he has also within him what we may describe as bodies appropriate to these various planes of nature, and consisting in each case of their matter. In the man's physical body there is etheric matter as well as the solid matter which is visible to us (see Plates XXIV. and XXV.); and this etheric matter is readily visible to the clairvoyant. In the same way a more highly developed clairvoyant who was capable of perceiving the more refined astral matter, would see the man represented at that level by a mass of that matter, which is in reality his body or vehicle as regards that plane; and exactly the same thing is true with regard to the mental plane in its turn. The soul of man has not one body, but many bodies, for when sufficiently evolved he is able to express himself on all these different levels of nature, and he is therefore provided with a suitable vehicle of the matter belonging to each, and it is through these various vehicles that he is able to receive impressions from the worlds to which they correspond.

We must not think of the man as creating these vehicles for himself in the course of his future evolution, for every man possesses them from the beginning, though he is by no means conscious of their existence. We are constantly using to a certain extent this higher matter within ourselves, even though it be unconsciously. Every time that we think, we set in motion the mental matter within us, and a thought is clearly visible to a clairvoyant as a vibration in that matter, set up first of all within the man, and then affecting matter of the same degree of density in the world around him. But before this thought can be effective on the physical plane it has to be transferred from that mental matter into astral matter; and when it has excited similar vibrations in that, the astral matter in its turn affects the etheric matter, creating sympathetic vibrations in it, and that in turn acts upon the denser physical matter, the grey matter of the brain.

So every time we think, we go through a much longer process than we know; just as every time we feel anything we go through a process of which we are quite unconscious. We touch some substance and feel that it is too hot, and we snatch away our hand from it instantaneously, as we think. But science teaches us that this process is not instantaneous, and that it is not the hand which feels, but the brain; that the nerves communicate the idea of intense heat to the brain, which at once telegraphs back along the nerve-threads the instruction to withdraw the hand; and it is only as a result of all this that the withdrawal takes place, which seems to us to be immediate. The process has a definite duration, which can be measured by sufficiently fine instruments; the rate of its motion is perfectly well defined and known to physiologists. Just in the same way thought appears to be an instantaneous process; but it is not, for every thought has to go through the stages which I have described. Every impression which we receive in the brain through the senses has to pass up through these various grades of matter before it reaches the real man, the ego, the soul within.

We have here a kind of system of telegraphy between the physical plane and the soul; and it is important to realise that this telegraph-line has intermediate stations. It is not only from the physical plane that impressions can be received; the astral matter within a man, for example, is not only capable of receiving a vibration from etheric matter and transmitting it to the mental matter, but it is also quite capable of receiving impressions from the surrounding matter of its own plane, and transmitting those through the mental body to the real man within. So the man may use his astral body as a means for receiving impressions from and observing the astral world which surrounds him; and in exactly the same way through his mental body he may observe and obtain information from the mental world. But in order to do either of these things, he must first learn how they are done; that is to say, he must learn to focus his consciousness in his astral body or in his mental body, just as it is now focussed in the physical brain. I have already treated this subject fully in my little book on *Clairvoyance*, so that I need do no more than refer to it here.

Although science is not yet prepared to admit the existence of these various planes or degrees of matter in nature, there is nothing in this hypothesis in the least contradictory to its teaching. It should always be remembered that all this is a matter of direct knowledge and certainty to those who are in the habit of studying it, although it is presented to the consideration of the world merely as a hypothesis; but even the man who approaches the subject for the first time must surely see that in suggesting this we are not in any way claiming faith in a miracle, but simply inviting investigation of a system. The higher grades of matter follow on in orderly sequence from those which we already know, so that though to some extent each plane may be regarded as a world in itself, it is yet also true that the whole is in reality one great world, which can be fully seen only by the highly-developed soul.

To aid us in our grasp of this, let us take an illustration which, although impossible in itself, may yet be useful to us as suggesting rather startling possibilities. Suppose that instead of the sight which we now possess, we had a visual apparatus arranged somewhat differently. <u>In the human eye we have both solid and liquid matter</u>; suppose that both these orders of matter were capable of receiving separate impressions, but each only from that type of matter in the outside world to which it corresponded. Suppose also that among men some possessed one of these types of sight and some another. Consider how very curiously imperfect would be the conception of the world obtained by each of these two types of men. Imagine them as standing on the sea-shore; one being able to see only solid matter, would be utterly unconscious of the ocean stretched before him, but would see instead the vast cavity of the ocean-bed, with all its various inequalities, and the fishes and other inhabitants of the deep would appear to him as floating in the air above this enormous valley. If there were clouds in the sky they would be entirely invisible to him, since they are composed of matter in the liquid state; for him the sun would be always shining in the day-time, and he would be unable to comprehend why, on what to us is a cloudy day, its heat should be so much diminished; if a glass of water were offered to him, it would appear to him to be empty.

Contrast with this the appearance which would be presented before the eyes of the man who saw only matter in the liquid condition. He would indeed be conscious of the ocean, but for him the shore and the cliffs would not exist; he would perceive the clouds very clearly, but would see almost nothing of the landscape over which they were moving. In the case of the glass of water he would be entirely unable to see the vessel, and would therefore be quite unable to understand why the water should so mysteriously preserve the special shape given to it by the invisible glass. Imagine these two persons standing side by side, each describing the landscape as he saw it, and each feeling perfectly certain that there could be no other kind of sight but his in the universe, and that anyone claiming to see anything more or anything different must necessarily be either a dreamer or a deceiver!

We can smile over the incredulity of these hypothetical observers; but it is exceedingly difficult for the average man to realise that, in proportion to the whole that is to be seen, his power of vision is very much more imperfect than either of theirs would be in relation to the world as he sees it. And *he* also is strongly disposed to hint that those who see a little more than he does must really be drawing upon their imagination for their alleged facts. It is one of the commonest of our mistakes to consider that the limit of our power of perception is also the limit of all that there is to perceive. Yet the scientific evidence is indisputable, and the infinitesimal proportion (as compared to the whole) of the groups of vibrations by which alone we can see or hear is a fact about which there can be no doubt. The clairvoyant is simply a man who developes within himself the power to respond to another octave out of the stupendous gamut of possible vibrations, and so enables himself to see more of the world around him than those of more limited perception.

Chapter IV

MAN'S VEHICLES

If we turn to Plate II. we shall see there a diagram of these planes of nature, and we shall also observe the names which have been employed to designate the vehicles or bodies of man which correspond to them. It will be noticed that the names used in Theosophical literature for the higher planes are derived from Sanskrit, for in Western philosophy we have as yet no terms for these worlds composed of finer states of matter. Each of these names has its especial meaning, though in the case of the higher planes it indicates only how little we know of those conditions.

Nirvâna has for ages been the term employed in the East to convey the idea of the highest conceivable spiritual attainment. (To reach Nirvâna was to pass beyond humanity, to gain a level of peace and bliss far above earthly comprehension.) So absolutely was all that was earthly left behind by the aspirant who attained

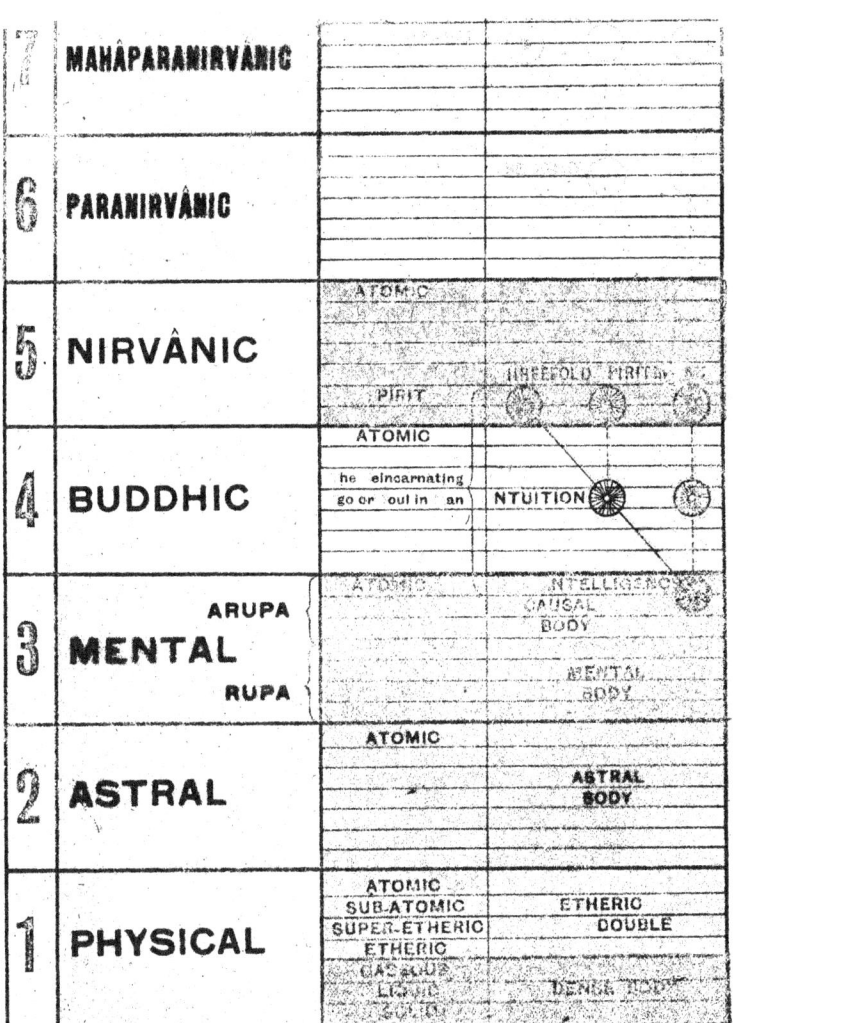

II.

conceivable spiritual attainment.

PLANES OF NATURE

7 MAHÂPARANIRVÂNIC	FIRST	TRIPLE MANIFESTATION	
6 PARANIRVÂNIC		SECOND	
5 NIRVÂNIC	ATOMIC	THIRD	
	SPIRIT	THREEFOLD SPIRIT in MAN	
4 BUDDHIC	ATOMIC		
	The Reincarnating Ego or Soul in Man	INTUITION	
3 MENTAL {ARUPA / RUPA}	ATOMIC	INTELLIGENCE / CAUSAL BODY	
		MENTAL BODY	
2 ASTRAL	ATOMIC	ASTRAL BODY	
1 PHYSICAL	ATOMIC / SUB-ATOMIC / SUPER-ETHERIC / ETHERIC	ETHERIC DOUBLE	
	GASEOUS / LIQUID / SOLID	DENSE BODY	

II.

its transcendent glory, that some European orientalists fell at first into the mistake of supposing that it was an entire annihilation of the man—an idea than which nothing could be more utterly the opposite of the truth. To gain the full use of the exalted consciousness of this exceedingly elevated spiritual condition is to reach the goal appointed for human evolution during this æon or dispensation—to become an adept, a man who is something more than man. For the vast majority of humanity such progress will be attained only after cycles of evolution, but the few determined souls who refuse to be daunted by difficulties, who as it were take the kingdom of heaven by violence, may find this glorious prize within their reach at a much earlier period.

Of the states of consciousness above this we naturally know nothing, except that they exist. "Para" signifies "beyond," and "Maha" means "great," so all the information conveyed by the names of these conditions is that the first is "the plane beyond Nirvâna," and the second is "the greater plane beyond Nirvâna"—showing that those who bestowed these appellations thousands of years ago either possessed no more direct information than we have, or else, possessing it, despaired of finding any words in which it could be expressed.

The name of Buddhi has been given to that principle or component part of man which manifests itself through the matter of the fourth plane, while the mental plane is the sphere of action of what we call the mind in man. It will be observed that this plane is divided into two parts, which are distinguished by a difference in colour and the names of "rupa" and "arupa," meaning respectively "having form" and "formless." These are names given in order to indicate a certain quality of the matter of the plane; in the lower part of it the matter is very readily moulded by the action of human thought into definite forms, while on the higher division this does not occur, but the more abstract thought of that level expresses itself to the eye of the clairvoyant in flashes or streams. A fuller account of this will be found in the sixth of our series of Theosophical manuals.

The name "astral" is not of our choosing; we have inherited it from the mediæval alchemists. It signifies "starry," and is supposed to have been applied to the matter of the plane next above the physical because of the luminous appearance which is associated with the more rapid rate of its vibration. The astral plane is the world of passion, of emotion and sensation; and it is through man's vehicle on this plane that all his feelings exhibit themselves to the clairvoyant investigator.) The astral body of man is therefore continually changing in appearance as his emotions change, as we shall show in detail later.

In our literature certain colours have usually been employed to represent each of the lower planes, following a table of colours given by Madame Blavatsky in her monumental work *The Secret Doctrine;* but it should be clearly understood that these are employed simply as distinctive marks—that they are merely symbolical, and are not in any way intended to imply a preponderance of a particular hue in the plane to which it is applied. All known colours, and many which are at present unknown to us, exist upon each of these higher planes of nature; but as we rise from one stage to another, we find them ever more delicate and more luminous, so that they might be described as higher octaves of colour. An attempt is made to indicate this in our illustrations of the various vehicles appropriate to these planes, as will be seen later.

It will be noticed that the number of planes is seven, and that each of them in turn is divided into seven sub-planes. This number seven has always been considered as holy and occult, because it is found to underlie manifestation in various ways. In the lower planes which are within the reach of our investigation the sevenfold subdivision is very clearly marked; and all indications seem to warrant the assumption that in those higher realms which are as yet beyond our direct observation a similar arrangement obtains, allowing for the difference of conditions.

As man learns to function in these higher types of matter, he finds that the limitations of the lower life are transcended, and fall away one by one. He finds himself in a world of many dimensions, instead of one of three only; and that fact alone opens up a whole series of entirely new possibilities in various directions. The study of these additional dimensions is one of the most fascinating that can be imagined; and those who feel an interest in it cannot do better than take it up in earnest, beginning with Mr. C. H. Hinton's admirable volumes of *Scientific Romances*. Short of really gaining the sight of the other planes, there is no method by which so clear a conception of astral life can be obtained as by the realisation of the fourth dimension.

It is not my object at the moment to describe all that is gained by the wonderful extension of consciousness which belongs to these higher planes—indeed, I have done that already to some extent in a previous book. For the present we need refer only to one line of investigation—that connected with the constitution of man, and how he came to be what he is.

The history of his earlier evolution can be obtained only by examination of those ineffaceable records of the past from which all that has happened since the solar system came into existence may be recovered, and caused to pass before the mind's eye; so that the observer sees everything precisely as though he had been present when it occurred, with the enormous additional advantage of being able to hold any single scene as long as may be required for careful examination, or to pass a whole century of events in review in a few moments if desired. This wonderful reflection of the divine memory cannot be consulted with perfect certainty below the mental plane, so for the ready reading of this earlier history it is necessary that the student should at least have learnt to use with freedom the senses of his mental body; and if he is so fortunate as to have under his control the faculties of the still higher causal body, his task will be easier still. The question of these records has been more fully dealt with in Chapter VII. of my little book on *Clairvoyance*, to which the reader may be referred for further details.

Chapter V

THE TRINITY

We must now endeavour to understand how man comes into existence amidst this wonderful system of the planes of nature, and in order to do that we shall find ourselves compelled to take an excursion into the domain of theology, though in such theology as interests us we deal with no pious opinions or speculations, but only with what to us is proved scientific fact.

When we search these records in order to discover the origin of man, what do we see? We find that man is the resultant of an elaborate and beautiful evolutionary scheme, and that in him three streams of Divine life may be said to converge. One of the sacred scriptures of the world speaks of God as having made man in His own image—a statement which, when it is properly understood, is seen to embody a great occult truth. All religions agree in describing the Deity as threefold in His manifestation, and it will be found that the soul of man is also threefold, and that there is the closest possible connection between these facts.

It will, of course, be understood that we are speaking now not of the Absolute, the Supreme, and the Infinite (for of Him naturally we can know nothing, except that He *is*), but of that glorious Manifestation of Him who is the great Guiding Force or deity of our own solar system —who is called in our philosophy the Logos of the system. Of Him is true all that we have ever heard predicated of the Deity—all that is good, that is, for in these days we hear so very much that is not good attributed to Him. Those who profess to worship Him frequently attribute to Him their own vices, and impiously dare to describe Him as jealous, angry, revengeful and cruel. Such abominable blasphemy may possibly be less heinous in the Central African savage, who has no conception of power except as expressed in cruelty and bloodthirstiness; but there can be no shadow of excuse for it among people who profess to be civilized, and those who so malign the Fount of all Goodness and Love are committing a crime whose evil results cannot easily be measured. But all that we have heard of God which is good—the love, the wisdom, the power, the patience and compassion, the omniscience, the omnipresence, the omnipotence—all of this, and much more, is true of the

Solar Logos, in whom, in very truth, we live and move and have our being. And be it remembered that in Theosophy we do not offer this as a pious opinion or an article of religious faith; to the clairvoyant investigator this Mighty Existence is a definite certainty—not that any merely human development can enable us directly to see Him, but that unmistakable evidence of His action and His purpose surrounds us on every side as we study the life of the higher planes.

As He shows Himself to us in His work the Solar Logos is undoubtedly triple—three and yet one, as religion has long ago told us. There is much that at first sight seems quite incomprehensible in the statements on this subject which are contained in the old formulæ of the Church; yet when explained by the light of the Theosophical teaching it will be seen that they constitute a remarkably accurate and very beautiful declaration of the truth, even though here and there passages of the most degraded materialism have crept in. The real beauty and meaning of the Athanasian Creed, for example, can be seen only when it is studied verse by verse with the aid of Theosophical diagrams.

It is obviously impossible to picture this divine manifestation in any way, for it is necessarily entirely beyond our power either of representation or comprehension, yet a small part of its action may perhaps to some extent be brought within our grasp by the employment of certain simple symbols, such as those adopted in Plate II. It will be seen that on the seventh or highest plane of our system the triple manifestation of our Logos is imaged by three circles, representing His three aspects. Each of these aspects appears to have its own quality and power. In the First Aspect He does not manifest Himself on any plane below the highest, but in the Second He descends to the sixth plane, and draws round Himself a garment of its matter, this making a quite separate and lower expression of Him. In the Third Aspect He descends to the upper portion of the fifth plane, and draws round Himself matter of that level, thus making a third manifestation. It will be observed that these three manifestations on their respective planes are entirely distinct one from the other, and yet we have only to follow up the dotted lines to see that these separate persons are nevertheless in truth but aspects of the one. Quite separate, when regarded as persons, each on his own plane—quite unconnected diagonally, as it were; yet each having his perpendicular connection with himself at the level where these three are one.

Thus we see a very real meaning in the

insistence of the Church "that we worship one God in Trinity, and Trinity in Unity, neither confounding the persons nor dividing the substance"—that is to say, never confusing in our minds the work and functions of the three separate manifestations, each on his own plane, yet never for a moment forgetting the Eternal Unity of the "substance," that which lies behind all alike on the highest plane.

It is instructive to notice here exactly the true meaning of this word person. It is compounded of the two Latin words *per* and *sona*, and therefore signifies "that through which the sound comes"—the mask worn by the Roman actor to indicate the part which he happened at the moment to be playing. Thus we very appropriately speak of the group of temporary lower vehicles which a soul assumes when he descends into incarnation as his "personality." Thus also these separate manifestations of the One on different planes are rightly thought of as persons.

Thus we see how it can be said:—"There is one Person of the Father, another of the Son, and another of the Holy Ghost; but the Godhead of the Father, of the Son, and of the Holy Ghost is all one—the glory equal, the majesty co-eternal." Truly the manifestations are distinct, each on its own plane, and consequently one appears lower than another; yet we have only to look back to the seventh plane to realise that "in this Trinity none is afore or after other, none is greater or less than another, but the whole three Persons are co-eternal together and co-equal." So also "every Person by himself is God and Lord," "and yet they are not three Lords, but one Lord."

See also how clear and luminous become many of the statements concerning the Second Aspect and His descent into matter. There is another and far wider meaning for this, as will be seen in Plate III.; but what is true of that grander descent is true also of this, for when we think of the Aspect on the higher plane as the essential Godhead ensouling the manifestation in matter relatively lower, though still high above our ken, we see how he is "God, of the substance of his Father, begotten before the world; but man, of the substance of his Mother, born in the world." For as an aspect of the divine He existed before the solar system, but His manifestation in the matter of the sixth plane took place during the life of that system.

So, "although he be God and Man, yet he is not two, but one Christ; one, not by conversion of the Godhead into flesh, but by taking of the manhood into God." One, that is, not only because of the essential Unity, but because of the glorious power of drawing back into Himself all that has been acquired by the descent into lower matter. But this belongs more especially to that greater descent illustrated for us in Plate III.

The greatest schism which has ever occurred in the Christian Church was that between the Eastern and Western branches, the Greek Church and the Roman. Although as a matter of fact political and financial considerations were largely responsible for this division, yet the doctrinal reason alleged for it was the supposed corruption of the truth, by the introduction into the Creed of the word *filioque* at the Council of Toledo in the year 589.

The question at issue was whether the Holy Ghost proceeded from the Father alone, or from the Father and the Son—surely a point sufficiently unpractical and remote from human knowledge to have been put aside by both parties for the sake of unity. But theological acrimony always seems to rage most bitterly around subjects the most obscure, unimportant, and uninteresting. Our diagram, however, does enable us to see what was the point at issue in this case; and furthermore, it shows us, curiously enough, that both parties were right, and that if they had only clearly understood the matter there need have been no schism at all.

The Latin Church held, quite reasonably, that there could be no manifestation on the fifth plane of a Force which admittedly came from the seventh, without a passage through the intermediate sixth, so they declared that He proceeded from the Father and the Son. The Greek Church, on the other hand, insisted absolutely on the distinctness of the Three Manifestations, and quite rightly protested against any theory of a procession from the First Manifestation through the Second such as would be typified in our diagram if we drew a diagonal line through the First, Second and Third. The dotted line on the right of Plate II., showing how the Third Aspect descends through the planes and finally manifests on the fifth, is of course the key to the true line of procession, and the absolute harmony of the two conflicting ideas.

The wonderful way in which man is made in the image of God may be seen by comparing the triad of the human soul with the Trinity in manifestation above it. So astonishingly material have been the orthodox conceptions, that this text has literally been interpreted as referring to the physical body of man, and made to mean that God created man's body in a shape which He foresaw as that which Christ would choose to assume when He came on earth—a rather remarkable instance of mental confusion even for a theologian.

A glance at Plate II. shows us at once the true meaning of those words. Not the physical body of man, but the constitution of his soul, reproduces with marvellous exactitude the method of Divine manifestation. Just as three aspects of the Divine are seen on the seventh plane, so the Divine Spark of the spirit in man is seen to be triple in its appearance on the fifth plane. In both cases the Second Aspect is able to descend one plane lower, and to clothe itself in the matter of that plane; in both cases the Third Aspect is able to descend two planes and repeat the process. So in both cases there is a Trinity in Unity, separate in its manifestations, yet one in the reality behind.

But for the moment we are concerned simply with the fact that each of the three Aspects or Persons or Manifestations of the Logos has an especial part to play in the preparation and development of the soul of man. What these parts are we shall endeavour to make clear by the help of the diagram given on Plate III. The horizontal subdivisions indicate the planes, precisely as in Plate II., and above them will be seen three symbols belonging to the series described by Madame Blavatsky in *The Secret Doctrine*. The highest represents the First

Aspect of the Logos, and bears only a central dot, signifying the primary manifestation in our system. The Second Aspect of the Logos is symbolized by a circle divided by a diameter, showing the dual manifestation which is always associated with the Second Person of any of the Trinities, while the lowest circle contains the Greek cross, one of the most usual symbols of the Third Aspect.

Chapter VI

THE EARLIER OUTPOURINGS

It is from this Third Aspect that the first movement towards the formation of the system comes. Previous to this movement we have in existence nothing but the atomic state of matter in each of the planes of nature, none of the aggregations or combinations which make up the lower sub-planes of each having yet been formed. But into this sea of virgin matter (the true Virgin Maria) pours down the Holy Spirit, the Lifegiver, as He is called in the Nicene Creed; and by the action of His glorious vitality the atoms are awakened to new powers and possibilities of attraction and repulsion, and thus the lower subdivisions of each plane come into existence. It will be seen that this is symbolized in the diagram by a line descending from the lowest circle straight through all the planes, growing broader and darker as it comes, to show how the Divine Spirit becomes more and more veiled in matter as it descends, until

THE EARLIER OUTPOURINGS 37

many are quite unable to recognise it as divine at all.

Yet the living force is nevertheless there, even when it is most strictly confined in the lowest of its forms. The recent experiments of Professor von Scbrön at Naples have conclusively proved the existence of life in the mineral kingdom, and show also in a most wonderful manner the action of the first and second of these great successive outpourings of the Divine Life.

Into this matter thus vivified, the second great outpouring of the divine life descends. Thus the Second Person of the Trinity takes form not of the "virgin" or unproductive matter alone, but of the matter which is already instinct and pulsating with the life of the Third Person, so that both the life and the matter surround Him as a vesture, and thus in very truth He is "incarnate of the Holy Ghost and the Virgin Mary," which is the true rendering of a prominent passage in our creed. (See *The Christian Creed*, page 42.)

Very slowly and gradually this resistless flood pours down through the various planes and kingdoms, spending in each of them a period equal in duration to one entire incarnation of a planetary chain, a period which, if measured as we measure time, would cover very many millions of years. This flood is symbolized in Plate III.

by the line which, starting from the second of the circles, sweeps down the left-hand side of the oval, gradually darkening as it approaches its nadir. After passing that point it commences its upward arc and rises through the physical, astral, and lower mental planes until it meets the third great outpouring, which is typified by the line starting from the highest circle and forming the right-hand side of the great oval. Of this meeting we shall say more hereafter, but for the moment let us turn our attention to the descending arc. To aid us the better to comprehend this, let us turn to Plate IV. This diagram, though it looks so different, in fact corresponds very closely with Plate III.; the variously coloured column on the left is identical with the downward-sweeping curve on our left in Plate III., and all the pyramidal figures which make the rest of the diagram are simply representations of the earlier part of the upward curve on the right of Plate III., pictured at various stages of its growth.

It will be observed that at various stages of its descent it is called by various names. As a whole, it is often spoken of as monadic essence, more especially when clothed only in the atomic matter of the various planes; but when on its downward course it energizes in the matter of the higher part of the mental

THE THREE OUTPOURINGS

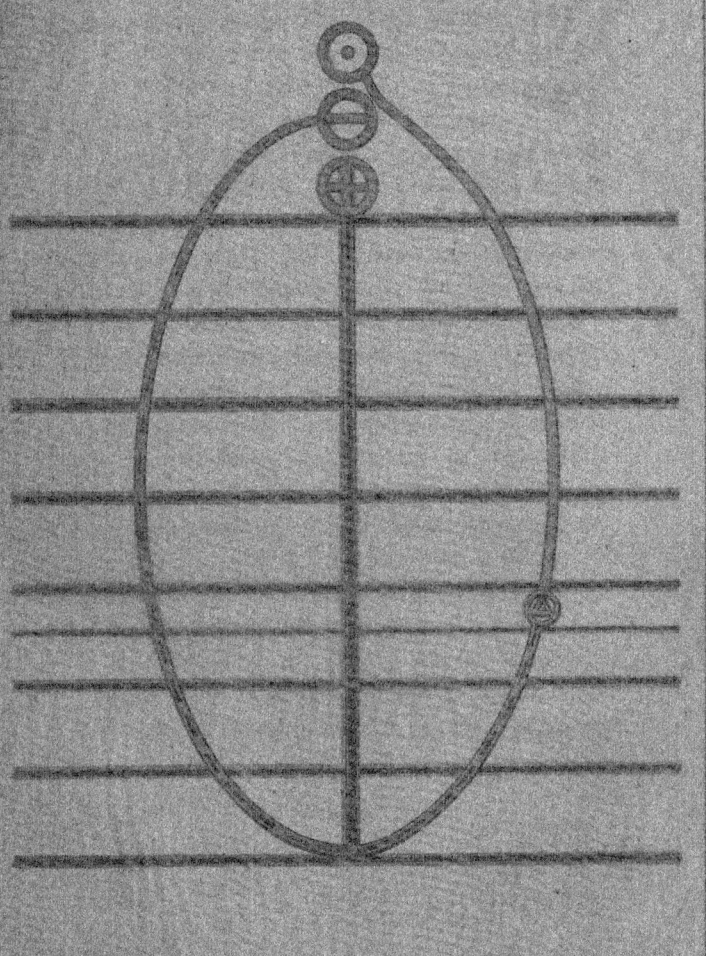

its upward arc and rises through the physical, astral, and lower mental planes until it meets the third great outpouring, which is typified by the line starting from the highest circle and forming the right-hand side of the great oval. Of this meeting we shall say more hereafter, but for the moment let us turn our attention to the descending arc. To aid us the better to comprehend this, let us turn to Plate IV. This diagram, though it looks so different, in corresponds very closely with Plate III.; variously coloured column on the left is identical with the downward-sweeping curve on our left in Plate III., and all the pyramidal figures which make the rest of the diagram are simply representations of the earlier part of the upward curve on the right of Plate III., pictured at various stages of its growth.

It will be observed that at various stages of its descent it is called by various names. As a whole, it is often spoken of as monadic essence, more especially when clothed only in the atomic matter of the various planes; but when on its downward course it energizes in the matter of the higher part of the mental

THE THREE OUTPOURINGS

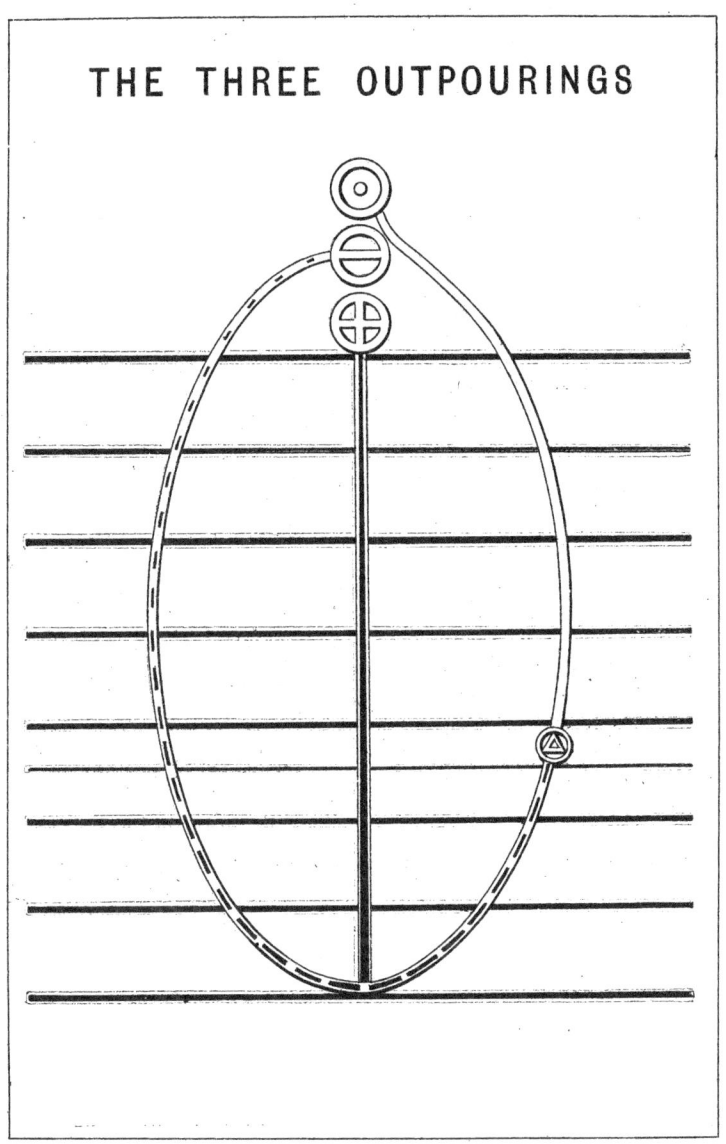

III.

plane, it is known as the First Elemental Kingdom. After spending a whole chain-period in that evolution, it descends to the lower or rupa levels of the same plane, and there it ensouls the Second Elemental Kingdom for another chain-period. Its next æon is spent on the astral level, where it is called the Third Elemental Kingdom, or very often simply elemental essence of the astral plane. At both of these stages it is very intimately connected with man, as it enters largely into the composition of his various vehicles, and influences his thought and action. This, however, is beside our present subject, and for a full description of this action of the "desire-elemental" and the "mental elemental" upon man we must refer our readers to other Theosophical works.

When this great life-wave of divine force reaches the lowest point of its destined course it is immersed in physical matter; and at this period, and for some time after it has begun its long upward journey, it is energizing or ensouling the mineral kingdom of the particular chain upon which it happens to be at the moment. At this stage it has sometimes been called "the mineral monad," just as at later periods of its evolution it has been named "the vegetable monad" and "the animal monad." But all these titles are somewhat misleading, because they seem to suggest that one great monad animates the entire kingdom.

Even when this monadic essence first comes before us, in the earliest of the elemental kingdoms, it is already not one monad, but very many—not one great life-stream, but many parallel streams, each possessing characteristics of its own. The whole scheme tends increasingly toward differentiation, and ever as these streams descend from kingdom to kingdom they divide and subdivide more and more. It may be that there is a point before all this evolution at which we may think of the great outpouring as homogeneous, though no man has ever seen it in that condition; and at the conclusion of the first great stage of evolution it is finally divided into individualities, each man being a separate soul, though as yet an undeveloped soul.

Now at all points between these two extremes its condition is something intermediate; there is always subdivision, but it is not yet carried to the point of individualization. It must never be forgotten that we are dealing all the while with the evolution of the ensouling force or life, and not of the outward form; and this ensouling energy evolves by means of the qualities acquired in physical incarnation. In the vegetable kingdom, for example, we have not a soul for one plant, but one group-soul for an enormous number of plants—perhaps in some cases for a whole species. In the animal kingdom this subdivision has proceeded much further, and though it may still be true among low forms of insect life that one soul animates many millions of bodies, in the case of the higher animals a comparatively small number of physical forms are the expression of one group-soul.

CHAPTER VII

THE ANIMAL GROUP-SOUL

THIS idea of the group-soul seems to many students novel and difficult; perhaps an Oriental simile may help us to understand it more readily. They tell us that the group-soul is like the water in a bucket, while if we suppose a tumblerful of water withdrawn from that bucket, we shall have a representation of the soul of the single animal. The water in the glass is for the time quite separate from that in the bucket, and it takes the form of the glass which contains it. Suppose that we put into that glass a certain amount of colouring matter, so that the water in it acquires a distinctive hue of its own; that colouring matter will represent the qualities developed in the temporarily separated soul by the various experiences through which it passes.

The death of the animal will be typified by pouring back the water from the glass into the bucket, when the colouring matter will at once spread through the whole of the water, tinting it faintly. In exactly the same way, whatever qualities have been developed during the life of the separated animal will be distributed through the whole group-soul after his death. It would be impossible to take again out of the bucket the same glass of water, but every glassful taken out afterwards will necessarily be coloured by the matter brought in from that first glass. If it were possible to take out of the bucket exactly the same molecules of water, to reproduce the first glassful exactly, that would be a veritable reincarnation; but since that is not possible, we have instead the reabsorption of the temporary soul into the group-soul—a process in which, nevertheless, everything that has been gained by the temporary separation is carefully preserved.

Not one glass at a time only, but many glasses simultaneously, are filled from each bucket; and each one of them brings back to the group-soul its own quota of evolved quality. Thus in time many different qualities are developed within each group-soul, and of course manifest themselves as inherent in every animal which is an expression of it. Hence come the definite instincts with which certain creatures are born. The duckling, the moment it is set free from the egg, seeks the water and can swim fearlessly, even though it may have been hatched by a hen which dreads water, and is terribly worried to find her charges rushing to what she supposes to be destruction. But that fragment of a group-soul which is functioning through the duckling knows perfectly well from previous experience that the water is its natural element, and the tiny body fearlessly carries out its behests.

All the while within each group-soul the tendency to further and further subdivision is steadily working. It manifests itself in a phenomenon which, though upon a higher plane, has a curious resemblance to the way in which a cell divides. In the group-soul, which may be thought of as vividly animating a great mass of matter on the mental plane, a kind of scarcely perceptible film appears, as we might suppose a sort of barrier gradually to form itself across the bucket. The water at first filters through this barrier to some extent, but nevertheless the glasses of water taken out from one side of that barrier are always returned to the same side, so that by degrees the water on one side becomes differentiated from the water on the other, and then the barrier gradually densifies and becomes impenetrable, so that we have eventually two buckets instead of one.

This process is constantly repeated, until by

the time that we reach the really higher animals a comparatively small number of bodies is attached to each group-soul. It is found that the individualization which lifts an entity definitely from the animal kingdom into the human, can take place only from certain types of animals. Only among domesticated creatures, and by no means among all classes of even those, does this individualization occur. It must of course be remembered that we are very little more than half through the evolution of this chain of worlds, and it is only at the end of this evolution that the animal kingdom is expected to attain humanity. Naturally, therefore, any animal which is now attaining or even approaching individualization must be very remarkably in advance of the others, and the number of such cases is consequently very small. Still they do occasionally occur, and they are of extreme interest to us as indicating the manner in which we ourselves came in existence in the remote past. The lunar animal kingdom, out of which we were individualized, was at a somewhat lower level than the animal kingdom of the present day; but the principle adopted seems to have been almost precisely the same.

Chapter VIII
THE UPWARD CURVE

BEFORE explaining this in detail we must refer once more to Plate IV. It will be remembered that the variously coloured bands which occupy the principal part of this diagram are intended to signify various stages in the upward progress of the monadic essence. In its downward course, which is indicated by the column to the left of the diagram, it simply aggregates round itself the different kinds of matter on the various planes, evolving that matter by accustoming and adapting it to convey vibrations and impressions, and at the same time acquiring for itself the power to receive and respond readily to these impressions at their respective levels. But when it has reached the lowest point of its immersion in matter, and turns to begin the grand upward sweep of evolution towards divinity, its work then is somewhat different. Its object then is to develope its consciousness fully at these various

INVOLUTION & EVOLUTION

SPIRIT

MAHĀPARANIRVĀNIC PLANE

PARANIRVĀNIC PLANE

NIRVĀNIC PLANE

BUDDHIC PLANE

MENTAL — ARUPA LEVEL / RUPA LEVEL

ASTRAL

PHYSICAL

MATTER — MINERAL. VEGETABLE. ANIMAL. HUMAN. SPIRITUAL.

IV.

Chapter VIII

THE UPWARD CURVE

Before explaining this in detail we must refer once more to Plate IV. It will be remembered that the variously coloured bands which occupy the principal part of this diagram are intended to signify various stages in the upward progress of the monadic essence. In its downward course, which is indicated by the column to the left of the diagram, it simply aggregates round itself the different kinds of matter on the various planes, evolving that matter by accustoming and adapting it to convey vibrations and impressions, and at the same acquiring for itself the power to receive respond readily to those impressions at their respective levels. But when it has reached the lowest point of its immersion in matter, and turns to begin the grand upward sweep evolution towards divinity, its work then is somewhat different. Its object then is velope its consciousness fully at these various

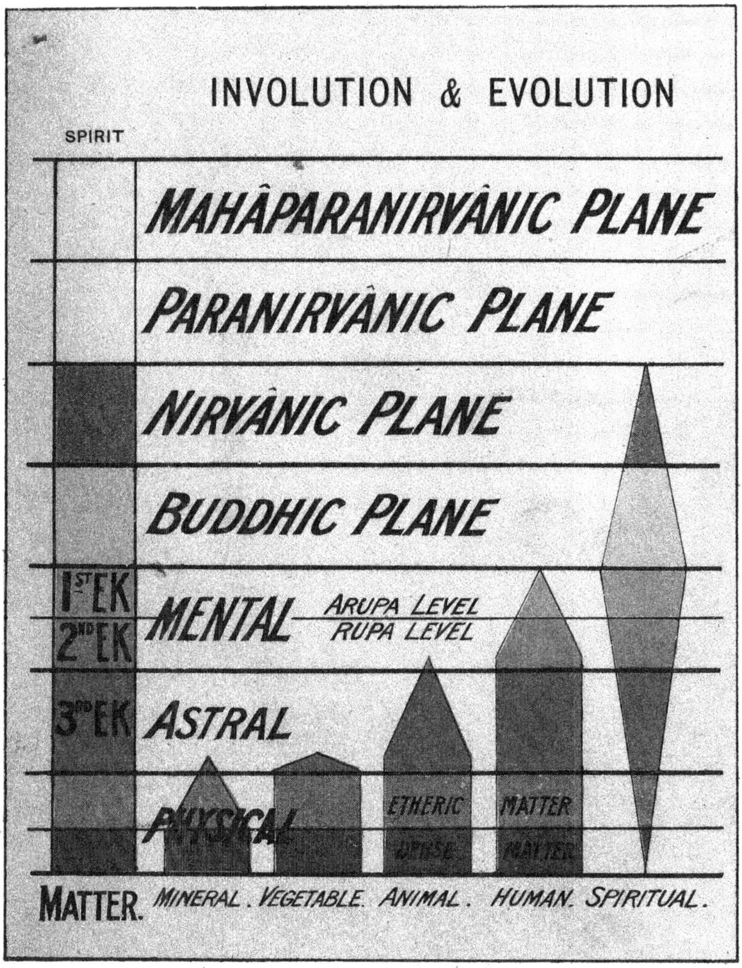

INVOLUTION & EVOLUTION

SPIRIT

MAHÂPARANIRVÂNIC PLANE

PARANIRVÂNIC PLANE

NIRVÂNIC PLANE

BUDDHIC PLANE

1ST EK — **MENTAL** — ARUPA LEVEL
2ND EK — RUPA LEVEL

3RD EK — *ASTRAL*

PHYSICAL — ETHERIC MATTER / DENSE MATTER

MATTER. MINERAL. VEGETABLE. ANIMAL. HUMAN. SPIRITUAL.

IV.

levels, learning to control the bodies which it constructs from them, and to use them definitely as vehicles, so that they shall not only serve as bridges to carry impressions from without to the soul, but shall also enable that soul to express itself on their several planes through their instrumentality.

In this effort it naturally begins with the lowest matter, since its vibrations, though they are the largest and coarsest, are also the least powerful or penetrating, and therefore the easiest to control. Thus it happens that man, although possessing in a more or less latent condition so many higher principles, is yet at first for a long time fully conscious only in his physical body, and afterwards very gradually developes the consciousness in his astral vehicle, while in his mental body it comes at a still later stage.

Turning to Plate IV. we see that we have a separate band or ribbon to represent each of the kingdoms. It will be noticed that in the band corresponding to the mineral kingdom we have the full width developed only in the denser part of the physical plane, and that in the part of the band which corresponds to etheric physical matter the band grows steadily narrower as we approach the higher planes. This of course indicates that in the mineral kingdom the control of the soul over the higher part of the etheric matter is not yet perfectly developed. It will be noticed also that there is a small point of red, showing that a certain amount of consciousness is already working through astral matter—that is to say, that a certain amount of desire is already manifesting itself.

It may seem strange to many people to speak of desire in connection with the mineral kingdom; but every chemist knows that in chemical affinity we have already a very distinct manifestation of preference on the part of various so-called elements; and what is that but a commencement of desire? One element has so strong a desire for the company of another that it will instantly forsake, in order to join it, any other substance with which it may happen to be in association. Indeed, it is by means of our knowledge of these likes and dislikes of the various elements that we obtain various gases when we want them. For example, oxygen and hydrogen are combined in water, but if we throw sodium into the water we shall find that oxygen likes sodium better than hydrogen, and promptly deserts the latter to combine with the former; so we have a compound called sodium hydroxide instead of water, and the released hydrogen escapes. Or if we put some zinc filings into diluted hydrochloric acid (which is hydrogen combined with chlorine) we find that the chlorine proceeds to abandon the hydrogen in order to join the zinc, so that zinc chloride remains, while hydrogen is given off and may be collected; in fact, this is one of the ordinary methods of obtaining it. So it will be seen that we are justified in speaking of the action of desire in the mineral kingdom.

If we now look at the band which symbolizes the vegetable kingdom we shall see that it is of full width not only in the dense physical, but also in the etheric part. We shall see also that the point indicating desire is more fully developed, indicating a far greater capacity of utilizing the lower astral matter. Those who have studied botany will be aware that likes and dislikes (that is to say, forms of desire) are very much more prominent in the vegetable world than in the mineral, and that many plants exhibit a great deal of ingenuity and sagacity in attaining their ends, limited though these ends may be as regarded from our point of view.

When we turn to the band representing the animal kingdom we find that consciousness has advanced very much further. It will be noticed that the band is of full width not only through the whole of the physical plane, but in the lowest sub-plane of the astral as well, showing that the animal is capable to the fullest possible extent of experiencing the lower desires, although the rapid narrowing of the band as we reach the higher sub-planes shows that his capacity for the higher desires is much more limited. Still it does exist; and so it happens that in exceptional cases he is capable of manifesting an exceedingly high quality of affection or devotion.

It will be observed also that the band representing the animal kingdom ends in a point of green, showing that at this stage there is already a development of intelligence, employing mental matter for its manifestation. It used at one time to be supposed that reason was the quality which distinguished man from the animals—that he possessed this faculty, while they had only instinct. As regards the higher domestic animals, however, that is certainly a mistake; anyone who has kept a dog or a cat, and made a friend of him (as assuredly anyone who keeps a pet animal ought to do) will surely have observed that such creatures undoubtedly do exercise the power of reason from cause to effect, although naturally the lines along which their reason can work are few and limited, and the faculty itself is far less powerful than ours. In the case of the average animal the point is quite correctly shown as embracing only the lowest variety of reason, acting in the matter of the lowest subdivision of the mental plane; but with the highly developed domestic animal the point might readily extend even to the highest of the four lower levels, though, of course it would remain only a point, and by no means the full width of the band.

Chapter IX

HUMAN CONSCIOUSNESS

WHEN we turn to the consideration of the band of colour which represents humanity, we at once note several quite new features. In this case the band retains its full width not only through the whole of the physical plane, but also through the whole of the astral, showing that a man is capable of all varieties of desire to the fullest possible extent, the highest as well as the lowest. It also exhibits the full width in the lowest level of the mental plane, indicating that as far as that level is concerned, man's reasoning faculty is fully developed. Higher than that, however, the development is not yet full; but an entirely new factor is introduced in the presence of the dark blue triangle on the higher mental plane, indicating the possession by the man of a causal body and a permanent reincarnating ego. This blue triangle corresponds to the other triangle in the circle which is seen in Plate III. In the case of the great majority of mankind the point which indicates consciousness of any sort upon the higher mental levels does not rise beyond the third or lowest of them. It is only very gradually, as his development progresses, that the ego is able to raise his consciousness to the second or the first of these sub-planes.

It is not, of course, implied that the man can function consciously at these heights as yet. In the lower types of men, desire is still emphatically the most prominent feature, though the mental development has also proceeded to some extent. Such a man during life would have a dim consciousness in his astral body while asleep, and after death he would be very fully conscious and active on the lower astral sub-planes. In fact, that lower astral life would probably form nearly the whole of the interval between his incarnations, for as yet he would have practically nothing of the life of the heaven-world. The consciousness of the man at this level is undoubtedly centred in quite the lower part of the astral body, and his life is principally governed by sensations connected with the physical plane.

The ordinary man of our own race is still living almost entirely in his sensations, although the higher astral is coming into play; but still for him the prominent question which guides his conduct is not in the least what is right or reasonable to do, but simply what he himself desires to do. The more cultured and developed among us are beginning to govern desire by reason—that is to say, the centre of consciousness is gradually transferring itself from the higher astral to the lower mental. Slowly as the man progresses it moves up further still, and the man begins to be dominated by principle rather than by interest and desire.

To be able to use these different bodies as definite vehicles in which the soul can consciously function is another and still greater development. Any fairly advanced and cultured man among the higher races of mankind has already consciousness fully developed in the astral body, and is perfectly capable of employing it as a vehicle if he were only in the habit of doing so. But to do this a definite effort would be necessary. The enormous majority of these men know nothing at all about the astral body or its uses, and so naturally make no effort of any kind. They have behind them the tradition of the immemorial custom of a long series of lives in which the astral faculties have not been used, for these faculties have been gradually and slowly growing inside a shell, something as a chicken grows inside the egg. The shell is composed of the great mass of self-centred thought in which the ordinary man is so hopelessly entombed. Whatever may have been the thoughts chiefly engaging his mind during the day, he usually continues them when falling asleep, and is thus surrounded by so dense a wall of his own making that he practically knows nothing of what is going on outside. Occasionally, but very rarely, some violent impact from without, or some strong desire of his own from within, may tear aside this curtain of mist for the moment and permit him to receive some definite impression; but even then the fog closes in again almost immediately, and he dreams on unobservantly as before. It is obvious that this shell may be broken in various ways.

First.—In the far distant future the slow but sure evolution of the man will undoubtedly gradually dissipate the curtain of mist, so that he will become conscious by degrees of the mighty world of intensely active life which surrounds him.

Secondly.—The man himself, having learnt the facts of the case, may by steady and persistent effort from within clear away the mist, and gradually overcome the inertia resulting from ages of inactivity. This is, of course, merely the hastening of the natural process, and will be in no way harmful if the man's development is proceeding with equal rapidity along other lines. But if he should gain this awakening without having attained at the same time the strength, knowledge and moral development which would naturally have preceded it, he would be liable to the double danger of misusing such powers as he might acquire, and of being overwhelmed by fear in the presence of forces which he could neither understand nor control.

Thirdly.—It may happen that some accident, or some unlawful use of magical ceremonies, may so rend the veil that it may never be wholly closed; and then the man is left in the terrible condition so well described by Madame Blavatsky in her story of "A Bewitched Life," or by Bulwer Lytton in his powerful novel *Zanoni*.

Fourthly.—Some friend who knows the man thoroughly, and believes him capable of facing the dangers of the astral plane and doing good unselfish work there, may act upon this cloud-shell from without and rouse the man to definite action. This is the awakening to which reference is made in our books, and naturally the man who does this undertakes a very serious responsibility towards the man whom he thus arouses. The elder worker assumes this responsibility only when by long and intimate acquaintance he has become reasonably certain that the younger possesses in some measure all the qualifications mentioned in Chapter XIV. of *Invisible Helpers;* but the need of helpers is so great that every aspirant may be absolutely certain that there will not be a day's delay in arousing him as soon as he is seen to be ready. Meantime any who feel themselves overlooked have always the resource of adopting the second method to which I referred above; but before doing so they would be well advised to assure themselves absolutely and beyond any possibility of doubt that they possess the requisite development along other lines, as otherwise their fall will be speedy and certain.

But, as has been explained in the books, a great deal of work may be done, and constantly is done, short of this full awakening. A man who falls asleep with the definite intention in his mind of doing a certain piece of work will assuredly go and attempt to carry out his intention as soon as he is freed from his physical body; but having done his best in connection with that particular case, he is almost certain to let the fog close round him once more, simply because of the fact that he has for ages been unaccustomed to initiate a fresh line of action when functioning apart from the physical brain. Many of our members make a practice of thus ensuring that they may perform at least one helpful action each night; and of course in many cases the action is such as to occupy the whole of the time spent in sleep, so that they are practically exerting themselves to the fullest extent possible for them. We should also remember that it is by no means only during sleep than we can give effective help; the strong living thought can be sent out at any moment, and can never fail in producing its effect. But the difference between the one who has been definitely awakened and the one who has not, is that in the case of the former the curtain of mist has been for ever dissipated, while in the latter it merely opens for the time and then shuts down as impenetrably as before.

CHAPTER X

THE THIRD OUTPOURING

IN order to understand the formation of the soul in man there is another great factor which must be taken into account. This is the third outpouring of the divine life, which comes from the first aspect of the Logos, and makes within each man that distinctive "spirit of the man which goeth upward" in contradistinction to "the spirit of the beast which goeth downward"—which, being interpreted, means that while the soul of the animal pours back after the death of the body into the group-soul or block to which it belongs, the divine spirit in man cannot so fall back again, but rises ever onward and upward towards the divinity from whom it came. This third wave of life is represented by the band on the right in Plate III., and it will be noticed that in this case the outpouring does not become darker or more materialized as it proceeds. Of itself it descends no lower than the buddhic plane, though its down-stretching points rest on the atomic mental. There it hovers like a mighty cloud, waiting for an opportunity of effecting a junction with the second outpouring, which is slowly rising to meet it. Although this cloud seems to exercise a constant attraction upon the essence below it, yet the development which makes the union a possibility must be made from below.

The illustration usually given in the East to help the neophyte to comprehend this process is that of the formation of the water-spout. There also we have a great cloud hovering above the sea, on the surface of which waves are constantly forming and moving. Presently a great finger is extended from the cloud—an inverted cone of violently whirling vapour. Underneath this a vortex is rapidly formed in the ocean, but instead of being a depression in its surface, as is the ordinary whirlpool, it is a whirling cone rising above that surface. Steadily the two draw closer and closer together, until they come so near that the power of attraction is strong enough to overleap the intervening space, and suddenly a great column of mingled water and vapour is formed where nothing existed before.

In just the same way the group-souls of the animal kingdom are constantly throwing parts of themselves into incarnation, like the temporary waves on the surface of the sea, and the process of differentiation continues until at last a time comes when one of these waves rises high enough to enable a down-stretching point from the hovering cloud to effect a junction with it, and it is then drawn up into a new existence neither in the cloud nor in the sea, but between the two and partaking of the nature of both. Thus it is separated from the group-soul of which hitherto it has formed a part, and falls back again into the sea no more.

Anyone who has made a friend of a really intelligent domestic animal will readily understand how this happens, for he will have seen the intense devotion manifested by the animal for the master whom he loves, and the great mental efforts which he makes to understand his master's wishes and to please him. Obviously both the animal's intellect and his power of affection and devotion will be enormously developed by these efforts; and the time will come when in this way he will raise himself so much above the general level of his group-soul that he will absolutely break away from it, and in doing so become a fit vehicle for this third outpouring, by the junction with which the individual is formed, which thereafter follows its own course of evolution back again to divinity.

It is sometimes asked why, if the essence was divine in the beginning, and returns again to divinity at the end—if the human monad was all-wise and all-good when it started on its long journey through matter—it was necessary for it to go through all this evolution, including as it does much sorrow and suffering, simply to return to its source in the end. But this question is based on a complete misconception of the facts. When what is sometimes, though perhaps inappropriately, called the human monad came forth from the divine it was not a monad at all—still less an all-wise and all-good one. There was no developed individualization in it—it was simply a mass of monadic essence. The difference between its condition when issuing forth and when returning is exactly like that between a great mass of shining nebulous matter and the solar system which is eventually formed out of it. The nebula is beautiful, no doubt, but vague and useless; the sun formed from it by slow evolution pours life and heat and light upon many worlds and their inhabitants.

Or we may take another analogy. The human body is composed of countless millions of tiny particles, and some of them are constantly being thrown off from it. Suppose that it were possible for each of these particles to go through some kind of evolution by means of which it would in time become a human being, we should not say that because it had been in a certain sense human at the beginning of that evolution, it had therefore not gained anything when it reached the end. The essence comes forth as a mere outpouring of force, even though it be divine force; it returns in the form of thousands of millions of mighty adepts, each capable of himself developing into a Logos.

It is this wonderful course of evolution that we shall try to indicate to a certain extent in our series of illustrations, and though the most that we can do is to endeavour to pourtray the change which takes place in the various vehicles of the man as he developes, it is yet hoped that some idea of the progress may thus be conveyed to those who are as yet unable to see. There is one point in connection with the junction which we have been trying to describe which requires further explanation. A curious change has taken place in the position of the monadic essence. All the way through its long ages of evolution in all the previous kingdoms, it has invariably been the ensouling and energizing principle—the force behind whatever forms it may have temporarily occupied. But now that which has hitherto been the ensouler becomes itself in turn the ensouled; from that monadic essence which was part of the animal group-soul is now formed the causal body—a splendid ovoid form of living light, into which the still more glorious light and life from above has descended, and by means of which that higher life is enabled to express itself as the human individuality.

Nor, as I have explained when writing upon this subject in *The Christian Creed*, should any think that it is an unworthy goal to reach as a result of so long and weary an evolution, thus to have become a vehicle of this last and grandest outpouring of the divine Spirit; for it must be remembered that without the preparation of this vehicle to act as the connecting link, the immortal individuality of man could never come into being. No fragment of the work which has been done through all these ages is lost, and nothing has been useless. For the upper triad thus formed becomes a transcendent unity, "not by conversion of the Godhead into flesh, but by taking of the manhood into God." Without that long course of evolution this final consummation could never have been reached, that man should rise to the level of divinity, and that thus the very Logos Himself should be made more perfect, in that He has of His own offspring those upon whom that love which is the essence of His divine nature has for the first time been fully lavished, and by whom it can be returned.

A stage of development much in advance of the ordinary man is typified for us by the band on the extreme right of the diagram in Plate IV. There we have the image of the highly spiritual man, whose consciousness has already evolved even beyond the causal body, so that he is able to function freely upon the buddhic plane, and has also a consciousness (at least when out of the body), upon a plane still higher than that, as is indicated by the lilac point. It will be seen that in his case the centre of consciousness (typified by the widest part of the ribbon) is not at all, as before, upon the physical and astral planes, but lies between the higher mental and the buddhic. The higher mental and the higher astral are in him much more developed than their lower parts, and although he still retains his physical body, as is shown by the fact that the lower point of the band still reaches the lowest physical limit, yet this *is* only a point, indicating that he holds this physical form merely for the convenience of working in it; and not in any way because his thoughts and desires are fixed there. He has long ago transcended all karma which could bind him to incarnation; and if he now takes upon himself the vehicles of the lower planes, it is simply in order that through them he may be able to work for the good of humanity, and to pour out at these levels influence which otherwise could not descend thereto. For the vibrations of certain types of the divine force are in themselves too fine to be appreciated by the grosser essence of these lower planes; but if they descend to them through the channel of one whose vehicles at these levels are perfectly pure, then they can be appreciated even down here, and so their work may be done.

When this causal body is newly formed it is transparent yet iridescent, like a gigantic soap-bubble, when viewed by the higher clairvoyant sight—that is to say, when examined at its own level by one who has fully developed the faculties of his own causal body, for it is only to such sight that it would be visible at all. But at this stage it also resembles the soap-bubble in being almost empty in appearance, for the divine force which is really contained within it has as yet had no time to develop its latent qualities by learning to vibrate in response to impacts from without, and consequently there is little colour to show. What little there is comes because certain qualities have been already evolved within the group-soul of which that causal body previously formed a part, and it is in process of communicating these to the force within, so that there is already a certain vibration at the rates corresponding to these; and consequently faint

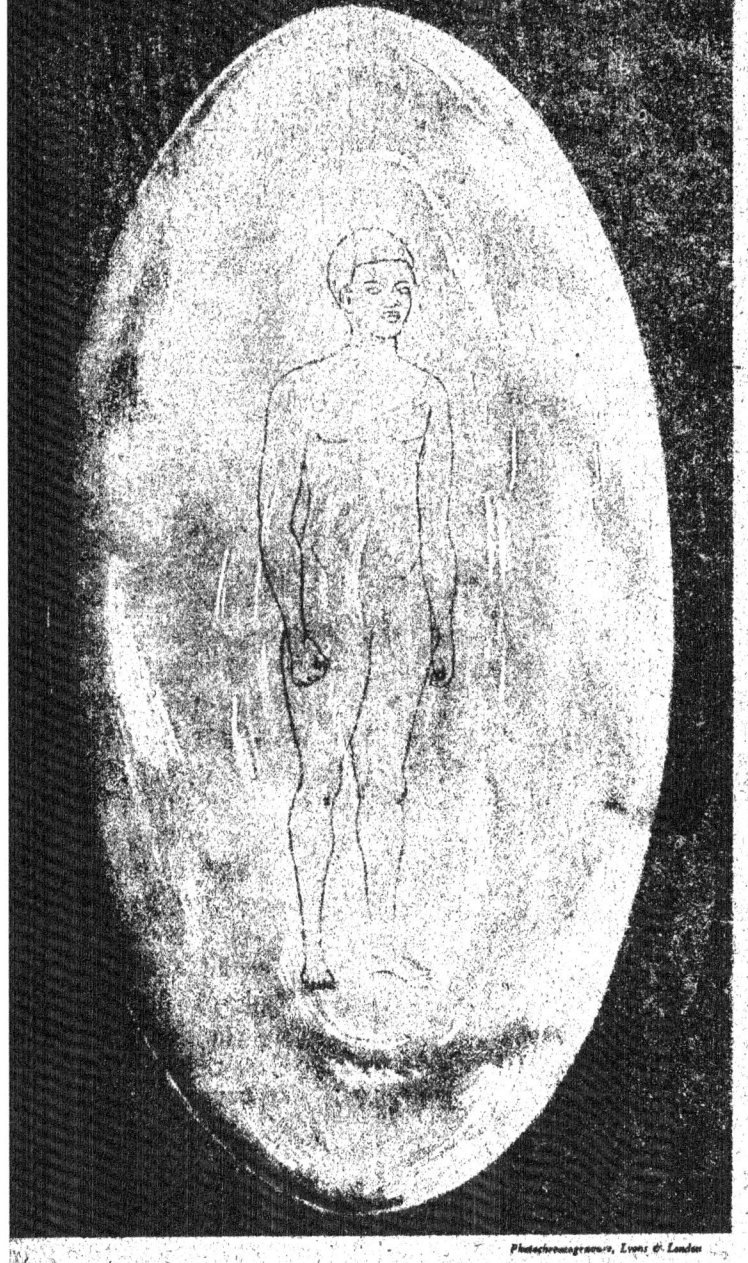

Photochromogravure, Lyons & London

V

levels influence which otherwise could not descend thereto. For the vibrations of certain types of the divine force are in themselves too fine to be appreciated by the grosser essence of these lower plane; but if they descend to them through the channel of one whose vehicles at these levels are ple... ..., then they can be appreciated ... ..., and so their work may begin.

When this causal body is first formed it is pure and yet irid....nt, like a ... soap-... ... viewed by the higher clairvoyant ... That is to say, when ... ... own looking one who has faint ... ... of his own causal body, one ... ... so light that it would ... ... at all. But at this stage it also res....b... the soap-bubble in being almost empty in appearance, for the divine force which is really contained within it has as yet had no time to develop its latent qualities by learning to ... ... response to impacts from without, and cons..., ently there is little colour to show. What little there is comes because certain qualities have been already evolved within the group-... of which that causal body previously formed a part, and it is in process of communicating these to the force within, so that there is already a certain vibration at the rates corresponding to these; and consequently faint

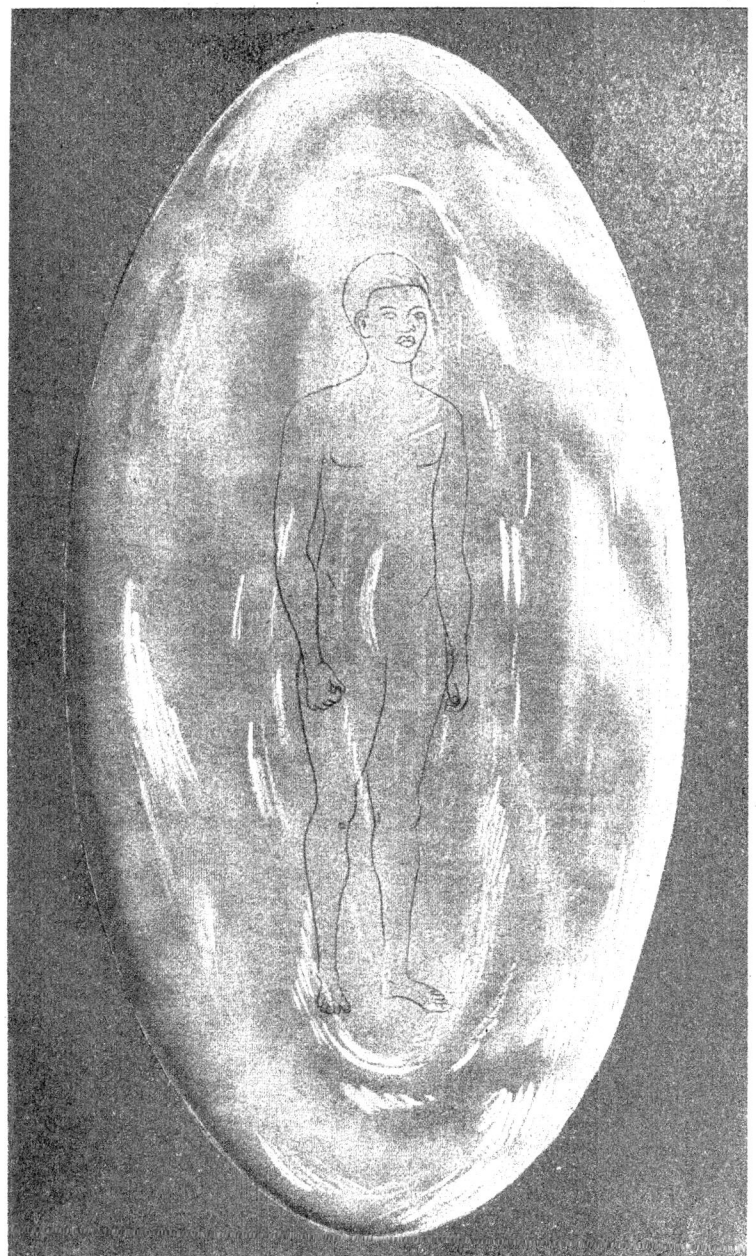

Photochromogravure, Lyons & London

V

indications of these rates of vibrations are even now observable within the form as dawning gleams of colour. Plate V. will give us some idea of its appearance at (or soon after) this stage, and it may be taken to represent the causal body of the primitive man. The grey shading at the left side of this illustration must not be taken as indicating any quality in the body; in fact it is not really present in it at all, but is introduced by the artist simply to give the effect of rotundity to the bubble.

But although the man now possesses a causal body, he is very far from being sufficiently conscious to receive or respond to impressions at that level; and since the appointed method for the evolution of his latent qualities is, as has been said, by means of impacts from without, it is obviously necessary that he should descend far enough to meet such impacts as can affect him. Therefore it is that the method of progress destined for him is that by reincarnation—that is to say, by putting forth part of himself into these lower planes for the sake of the experience to be gained there, and of the qualities which that experience developes, and then withdrawing back again into himself, bearing with him the results of his endeavour. Indeed, this putting forth of a part of himself into incarnation may be not inaptly likened to an investment; he expects, if all goes well, to reclaim not only the whole of his capital but also a considerable amount of interest, and he usually obtains this. But as with other investments, there is occasionally an opportunity of loss as well as of gain; for it is possible that some portion of that which he puts down may become so entangled with the lower matter through which it has to work, that it may be impossible wholly to reclaim it. The consideration of how this may happen hardly belongs to our present subject, but it will be found fully explained in *The Astral Plane*, p. 50.

It is not my purpose here to present the numerous arguments in favour of the doctrine of reincarnation. Those will be found fully detailed in the second of our Theosophical Manuals. In this book I am simply endeavouring to deal with the facts as seen, for it must be remembered that this process of reincarnation can be followed through all its stages by sufficiently developed clairvoyance, and that therefore for many Theosophical students it is not a hypothesis, but a matter of direct knowledge.

The soul puts himself down under the impulse of what in the East is called *Trishna*, the thirst for manifested existence, the desire to feel himself alive. He plunges about in the sea of matter, he strengthens self by selfishness, and shows himself to astral vision under the very unlovely guise depicted in Plate VII. Very gradually he learns that there is a higher evolution, and that the strong shell of selfishness (which was necessary for the formation of a powerful centre) becomes a hindrance to the growth of that centre after it has once been formed, and so must be broken up and thrown aside. Slowly through many incarnations his astral presentment developes from that of Plate VII. to that of Plate X., and later still to that of Plate XXIII. We shall try to follow this evolution, and illustrate it at its different stages.

Chapter XI

HOW MAN EVOLVES

He puts himself down first into the matter nearest to him, that of the lower levels of the mental plane. Immediately, and in a certain sense automatically, a vesture of this matter is drawn round him, a vesture which is an exact expression of such qualities as already exist in him, so far at least as they can be expressed at that level.

For it must never be forgotten that each stage in the descent means submission to limitation, and that consequently no expression of the soul upon any lower level can ever be a perfect expression. It is merely an indication of its qualities, just as a picture painted by an artist is a representation in two dimensions of a scene existing (or imagined as existing) in three dimensions. The picture represents the scene as nearly as it can be represented on a flat surface by means of perspective, but in reality almost every line and angle in it must of necessity be unlike the line or angle which it is intended to image. In exactly the same way the true quality as it exists in the soul cannot be expressed in matter of any lower level; the vibrations of the lower matter are altogether too dull and sluggish to represent it, the string is not sufficiently stretched to enable it to respond to the note which resounds from above. It can, however, be tuned to correspond with it in a lower octave, like a man's voice singing in unison with a boy's, expressing the same sound as nearly as the capabilities of the inferior organism permit.

Thus the colour which expresses a certain quality in the causal body will express it also in the mind body and even in the astral body, but the colour will be less delicate, less luminous and ethereal as we descend. The difference between these octaves of colour is very far greater than can be in any way represented upon paper or canvas; we can endeavour to image it only by stages or qualities, for even the next octave above the physical is entirely beyond the conception of our mind as long as it works under the limitation of the physical brain. The lowest astral colours may be thought of as dark and coarse, and they certainly are so as compared to the higher and purer hues, but at least they are luminous in their coarseness;

they are not so much dark *colour* in our ordinary sense of the word, as dimly-glowing fire.

At each stage as we ascend we shall find that while the higher matter exhibits a splendid power of expression of the nobler qualities, it gradually loses the power to express some which are lower. The peculiarly unpleasant hue which represents coarse sensuality in the astral body is quite incapable of reproducing itself in mental matter. It may be objected that this surely should not be so, as a man may undoubtedly have a sensual thought; but this idea does not seem accurately to represent the facts. A man may form a mental image which evokes sensual feeling in him, but the thought and the image will express themselves in astral matter, and not in mental. It will leave a very definite impression of its peculiar hue upon the astral body, but in the mental body it will intensify the colours which represent its concomitant mental evils of selfishness, conceit and deception. These in their turn will find no expression whatever in the resplendent glory of the causal body, but every intensification of them in the lower vehicle, every indulgence in them down here, tends somewhat to dim the luminosity of the colours representing the development of the opposite virtues in that higher existence which is so much nearer to reality.

The process by which the colours are produced works always from below upward. The man feels some impact from without, and in response to it a wave of emotion of some sort is awakened within him. That means that for the moment, while the emotion endures, the particular type of vibration (which represents it) is predominant in the astral body, as will presently be shown in our illustrations. After a time the emotion dies down, and the colour representing it fades away—but not entirely. A certain proportion of the matter of the astral body is normally vibrating at the especial rate appropriate to that emotion, and every great outburst of it adds somewhat to this proportion.

For example, most ordinary men have within them a certain amount of irritability, which expresses itself in the astral body as a scarlet cloud. When the man manifests that irritability by some special outburst of temper the whole astral vehicle is temporarily suffused with scarlet, as will presently be shown. The fit of passion subsides, and the scarlet flush dies away, but it has left its traces behind, for there is a slight permanent addition to the size of the scarlet cloud of irritability, and the whole matter of the astral body is a little more ready than before to respond to the vibration of anger when any opportunity offers. Naturally, exactly the same course is followed in the case of any other emotion, whether it be good or bad; and thus we see the clear manifestation in matter of the moral law, that every time we yield to a passion of any kind, we make it a little more difficult for ourselves to resist its next attack; while every successful effort at its repression makes the next victory a little easier.

The comparatively permanent colour in the astral body means a persistent vibration, which in course of time produces its due effect upon the mental body also, creating a vibration of similar character at that much higher level— provided, that is, that the vibration is of such a character as can be reproduced in that finer matter. It is by the same method of exciting sympathetic vibration that the higher qualities developed by the life on lower planes are gradually built into the causal body itself, though at that level, fortunately for us, only the effect of the loftier emotions can be recorded.

So, in the course of his many lives, man developes within himself many qualities, some good, some evil; but while all good development is steadily stored up and accumulated within the causal body, that which is evil can express itself only through the lower vehicles, and so is comparatively impermanent. Under the mighty law of divine justice, every man receives absolutely the exact results of his own action, whether it be bad or good; but the evil necessarily works out its effects upon the lower planes, because it is only in the matter of those planes that its vibrations can be expressed, and it has no overtones capable of awakening a response in the causal body. Its force, therefore, is all expended at its own level, and it reacts in its entirety upon its creator in his astral and physical life, whether it be in this or in future incarnations.

The good action or thought produces its results upon these lower planes too, but in addition to that it has the immensely higher and permanent effect upon the causal body which is so prominent a factor in the evolution of man. Thus, while all alike produce their results down here, and manifest them in the various temporary vehicles, it is the good qualities only which are retained as so much definite gain to the real man. The evil meets him again and again on his successive descents into incarnation, until he has vanquished it, and finally rooted out from his vehicles all tendency to respond to it—until, in fact, he is no longer liable to be swept away by any passion or desire, but has learnt to rule himself from within.

Chapter XII

WHAT HIS BODIES SHOW US

THIS process of learning is a gradual one, and the earlier manifestations of the undeveloped man upon the lower planes are by no means beautiful to see. We have not chosen absolutely the primitive man for illustration, because in his case there is as yet so very little to illustrate; but the savage whose causal body is represented in Plate V. would be likely to possess much such a mental body as is shown in Plate VI., and an astral body of the type given in Plate VII.

It must be understood that all these bodies occupy the same space, and interpenetrate one another; so that in looking clairvoyantly at the savage we should observe his physical body surrounded by a luminous ovoid mist, but that mist would present to us the appearance of Plate V., Plate VI., or Plate VII., according to the type of clairvoyance which we employed. Using our own astral senses, we should see his astral body only, and should learn from that what passions or emotions or sensations he was at the moment experiencing, and to which of these he was in the habit of yielding himself frequently. This is the field of the manifestation of desire—the mirror in which every feeling is instantly reflected, in which every thought even which has in it anything that touches the personal self must express itself. From its material a bodily form is given to the dark elementals which men create and set in motion by evil wishes and malicious feelings; from it also are bodied forth the beneficent elementals called into life by good wishes, gratitude and love.

As might naturally be expected, there is little of permanency about its manifestations; its colours, its brilliancy, the rate of its pulsations, are all changing from moment to moment. An outburst of anger will charge the whole astral body with deep-red flashes on a black ground; a sudden fright will instantaneously veil everything in a mist of ghastly, livid grey. Nevertheless, there will be moments when even this fluctuating astral vehicle is comparatively at rest, and it will then show a definite group of colours which retain more or less the same arrangement. Such a moment is that chosen for our illustration in Plate VII., and from this, as we shall presently see, a good deal of information about the man may be obtained.

Using our mental sight, it would be the mental body of our savage friend that we should perceive, and it would probably resemble that illustrated in Plate VI. As far as its colours are the same, this body would agree fairly with the astral in a condition of repose, but it would also be much more than this, for in it would appear whatever might be developed in the man of spirituality and intellectuality— not much yet, perhaps, in the case of our savage, but of considerable importance later on, as we shall see in due course. From this mental body we are therefore able to deduce what kind of man he is, and what sort of use he has made of his life so far in this incarnation.

But if we are fortunate enough to be able to apply to the problem the perfect power of vision exercised through our causal body, then what we see is the causal body of the savage, and from that we know how far his real life as a soul has advanced, and what progress the ego has made in its unfoldment towards divinity. It will be seen that, before the trained clairvoyant who is able to employ all these various degrees of sight in turn, the entire life of the man in all its stages lies open like a book; for on these higher planes no man can hide or disguise himself;

what he truly is, that he is seen to be by any unprejudiced spectator.

Unprejudiced, I say; because we must never forget that each sees the other through the medium of his own vehicles, and so is somewhat in the position of one looking at a landscape through coloured glass. Until he has learnt to make allowance for this influence, he will be liable to consider as most prominent in the man at whom he is looking just those characteristics to which he finds himself most ready to respond; but with a little careful practice he soon frees himself from the distortion produced by this personal equation, and is able to read clearly and accurately.

Chapter XIII

COLOURS AND THEIR MEANING

BEFORE we can intelligently study the detail of these various bodies, we must familiarize ourselves with the general meaning of the various shades of colour in them, as indicated in our frontispiece. It will be realised that almost infinite variety is possible in their combination. I am endeavouring to give, as nearly as possible, the exact shade which expresses the unmixed emotion whose name is attached to it; but human emotions are hardly ever unmixed, and so we have constantly to classify or to analyse indeterminate hues in the formation of which many factors have played their part.

Anger, for example, is represented by scarlet, and love by crimson and rose; but both anger and love are often deeply tinged with selfishness, and just so far as that is the case will the purity of their respective colours be dimmed by the hard brown-grey which is so characteristic of this vice. Or again, either of them may be mingled with pride, and that would instantly show itself by a tinge of deep orange. Many examples of such commingling, and of the resultant shades of colour, will be seen as we continue our investigation; but our first endeavour must be to learn to read the meaning of the simpler hues. We will give here a list of some of these which are most common.

Black.—Thick black clouds in the astral body indicate hatred and malice. When a person unhappily gives way to a fit of passionate anger, the terrible thought-forms of hate may generally be seen floating in his aura like coils of heavy, poisonous smoke.

Red.—Deep-red flashes, usually on a black ground, show anger; and this will be more or less tinged with brown as there is more or less of direct selfishness in the type of anger. What is sometimes called "noble indignation" on behalf of some one oppressed or injured may express itself in flashes of brilliant scarlet on the ordinary background of the aura.

Lurid, sanguinary red—a colour which is quite unmistakable, though not easy to describe —indicates sensuality.

Brown.—Dull brown-red, almost rust-colour, shows avarice; and it usually arranges itself in parallel bars across the astral body, giving a very curious appearance.

Dull, hard brown-grey signifies selfishness, and is unfortuately one of the very commonest colours in the astral body.

Greenish-brown, lit up by deep red or scarlet flashes, denotes jealousy, and in the case of the ordinary man there is nearly always a good deal of this colour present when he is what is called "in love."

Grey.—Heavy leaden grey expresses deep depression, and where this is habitual its appearance is sometimes indescribably gloomy and saddening. This colour also has the curious characteristic of arranging itself in parallel lines, as has that of avarice, and both give the impression that their unfortunate victim is imprisoned within a kind of astral cage.

Livid grey, a most hideous and frightful hue, shows fear.

Crimson.—This colour indicates love, and is often the most beautiful feature in the vehicles of the average man. Naturally it varies very greatly with the nature of the love. It may be dull, heavy and deeply tinged with the brown of selfishness, if the so-called love occupies itself chiefly with the consideration of how much affection is received from somebody else, how much return it is getting for its investment. But if the love be of that kind that thinks never of itself at all, nor of what it receives, but only of how much it can give, and how entirely it can pour itself forth as a willing sacrifice for the sake of the loved one, then it will express itself in the most lovely rose-colour; and when this rose-colour is exceptionally brilliant and tinged with lilac, it shows the more spiritual love for humanity. The intermediate possibilities are countless; and the affection may of course be tinged in various other ways, as by pride or jealousy.

Orange.—This colour is always significant of pride or ambition, and has almost as many variations as the last-mentioned, according to the nature of the pride or the ambition. It is not infrequently found in union with irritability.

Yellow.—This is a very good colour, implying always the possession of intellectuality. Its shades vary very much, and it may be much complicated by the admixture of various other hues. Generally speaking, it has a deeper and duller tint if the intellect is directed chiefly into lower channels, most especially if the objects are selfish; but it becomes brilliantly golden, and rises gradually to a beautiful clear and luminous lemon or primrose yellow, as it is addressed to higher and more unselfish objects.

Green.—No colour has more varied signification than this, and it requires some study to interpret it correctly. Most of its manifestations indicate a kind of adaptability, at first evil and deceitful, but eventually good and sympathetic.

Grey-green, a peculiar shade of it which can hardly be described otherwise than by the epithet "slimy," signifies deceit and cunning, and will be found very prominently in the astral body of most savages. Unfortunately it is by no means rare among more civilised men, who ought long ago to have passed the stage of evolution which it indicates. As the man advances, this hue improves into a bright emerald-green, which still means versatility, ingenuity and quickness of resource, but no longer implies any evil intent in connection with these qualities. It indicates the power of "being all things to all men," not now for the purpose of tricking or misleading them, but at first in order to please them, to obtain their praise or their favour, and later on, as understanding developes, for the purpose of helping and strengthening them. Eventually it becomes a lovely pale, luminous blue-green, such as may sometimes be seen in an exceptionally delicate sunset sky, and then it shows some of the grandest qualities of human nature, the deepest sympathy and compassion, with the power of perfect adaptability which they only can give. In its earlier developments a bright apple-green seems always to accompany strong vitality.

Blue.—Dark, clear blue usually indicates religious feeling, but this also varies immensely according to the type of the feeling, its purity or bigotry, its selfishness or nobility. It is liable to be tinted by almost any of the qualities previously mentioned, so that we may have any shade from indigo on one side and rich deep violet on the other, down to a muddy grey-blue which is at the level of the African's fetish-worship. The tinge of love or fear, of deceit or of pride, may mingle with the hue of religion, and thus there is a wide range of variation observable.

Light blue, such as ultramarine or cobalt, shows devotion to a noble spiritual ideal, and gradually rises to a luminous lilac-blue, which indicates the higher spirituality, and is usually accompanied by sparkling golden stars, representing elevated spiritual aspirations.

It is easy to understand how almost infinite may be the combinations and modifications of all these hues, so that the most delicate gradation of character or the most evanescent of mingled feelings is expressed with the greatest accuracy. The general brilliancy of the astral body, the comparative definiteness or indefiniteness of its outline, and the relative brightness of the different centres of force, are all points which have to be taken into consideration in reading the full meaning of what is seen. Another fact worth mentioning is that developed or developing psychical faculties show themselves by means of the colours which lie beyond the visible spectrum, so that it is impossible to picture them with physical hues. The ultra-violet tints denote the higher and purer developments, while gruesome combinations of the ultra-red reveal the wickedness of the dabbler in evil and selfish forms of magic. Occult advancement shows itself not only by these colours, but also by the greater luminosity of the various bodies, by their increased size and more definite outline, as will presently be seen in our illustrations.

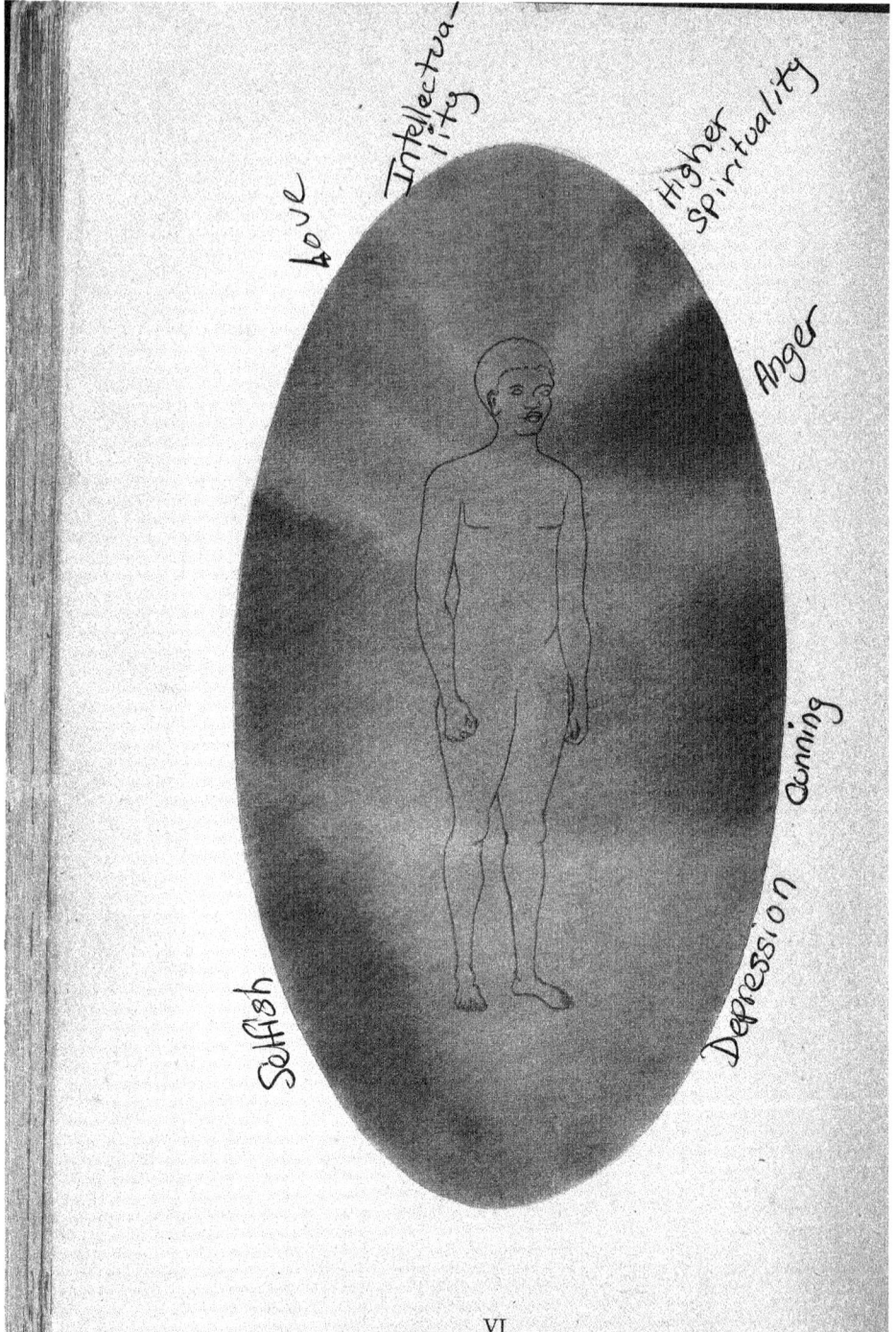

CHAPTER XIV

THE SAVAGE

APPLYING this information to the consideration of the mind-body of our savage in Plate VI., certain facts about the man at once become obvious. Although on the whole it is a very poor and undeveloped mind-body, yet some progress has already been made. The dull yellow at the top indicates a certain amount of intellect, but also shows by the muddiness of the colour that it is applied exclusively to selfish ends. The devotion denoted by the gray-blue must be a fetish-worship, largely mixed with fear, and prompted by considerations of self-interest; while the muddy crimson on our left suggests a commencement of affection which must as yet be principally selfish also. The band of dull orange testifies pride, but of quite a low order; while the large flash of scarlet expresses a strong tendency to anger, which would evidently blaze out upon very slight provocation. The broad band of dirty green which occupies

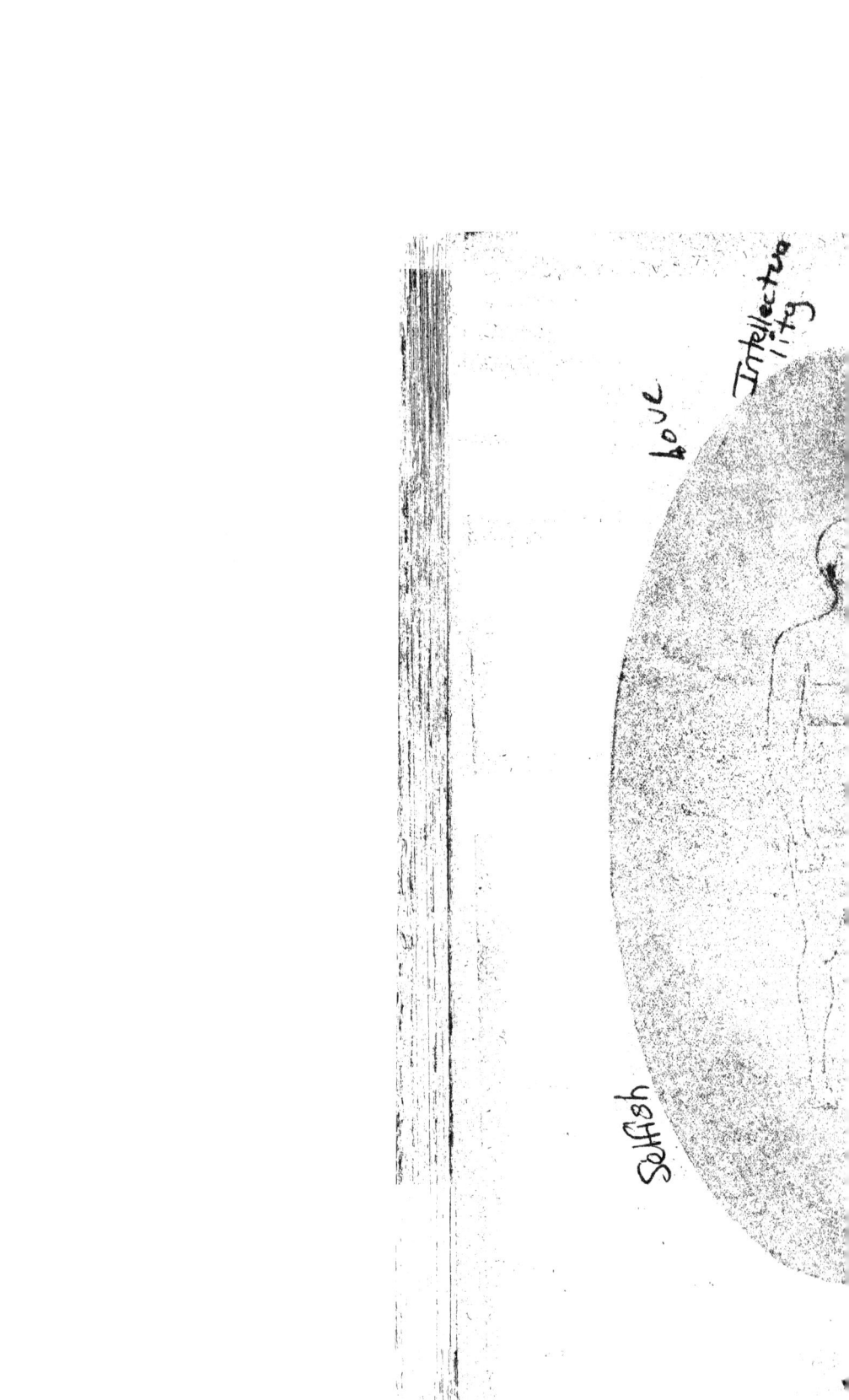

CHAPTER XIV

THE SAVAGE

APPLYING this information to the consideration of the mind-body of our savage in Plate VI., certain facts about the man at once become obvious. Although on the whole it is a very poor and undeveloped mind-body, yet some progress has already been made. The dull yellow at the top indicates a certain amount of intellect, but also shows by the muddiness of the colour that it is applied exclusively to selfish ends. The devotion denoted by the gray-blue must be a fetish-worship, largely tinged with fear, and prompted by considerations of self-interest; while the muddy crimson on our left suggests a commencement of affection which must as yet be principally selfish also. The band of dull orange implies pride, but of quite a low order; while the large dash of scarlet expresses a strong tendency to anger, which would evidently blaze out upon very slight provocation. The broad band of dirty green which occupies so great a portion of the body shows forth deceit, treachery and avarice—the latter quality being indicated by the brownish tint which is observable. At the bottom we notice a sort of deposit of mud colour, suggesting general selfishness and the absence of any desirable quality.

It is just that absence of any well-defined higher quality which makes us certain that, in turning to the corresponding astral body (Plate VII.) we shall find it almost entirely uncontrolled. Accordingly, we see how enormous a proportion of this vehicle of desire is occupied exclusively by sensuality, indicated by the very unpleasant brown-red which is almost blood-colour. It is not easy to reproduce the peculiar lurid tinge given by this quality, which is so painfully common except among the more advanced souls.

Deceit, selfishness and greed are conspicuous here, as might be expected, and fierce anger is also implied by the smears and blots of dull scarlet. Affection is scarcely indicated at all, and such intellect and religious feeling as appear are of the lowest possible kind.

Another point which should be noticed is the irregularity of the outline of this astral body, the generally blurred effect, and the manner in which the colours are arranged. As we pass to the vehicles of the more evolved human beings

VII

so great a portion of the body shows forth deceit, treachery and avarice—the latter quality being indicated by the brownish tint which is observable. At the bottom we notice a sort of deposit of mud colour, suggesting general selfishness and the absence of any desirable quality.

It is just that absence of any well-defined higher quality which makes us certain that, in turning to the corresponding astral body (Plate VII.) we shall find it almost entirely uncontrolled. Accordingly, we see how enormous a proportion of this vehicle of desire is occupied exclusively by sensuality, indicated by the very unpleasant brown and which is almost blood-red or. It is not easy to reproduce the peculiar sordid tinge given by this quality, which is so painfully common except among the more advanced souls.

Deceit, selfishness and greed are conspicuous here, as might be expected, and fierce anger is also implied by the smears and blots of dull scarlet. Affection is scarcely indicated at all, and such intellect and religious feeling as appear are of the lowest possible kind.

Another point which should be noticed irregularity of the outline of this astral the generally blurred effect, and the manner in which the colours are arranged. As we pass to the vehicles of the more evolved human beings

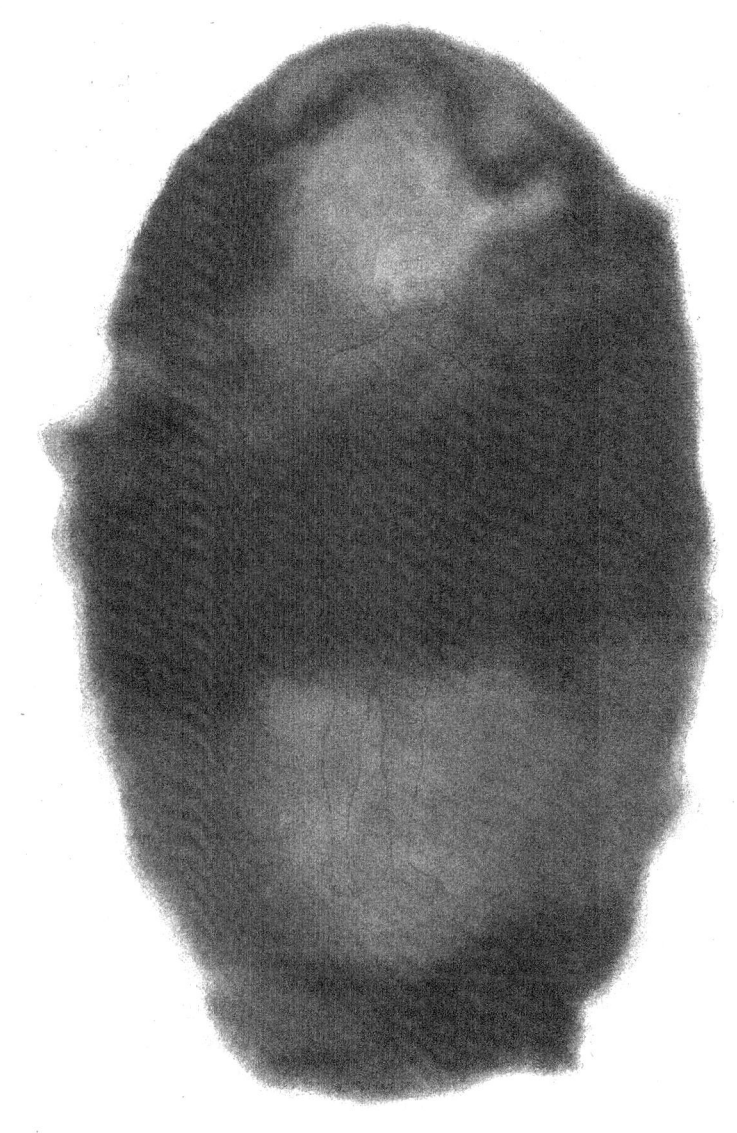

VII

we shall find a considerable improvement in this respect. The colours always to some extent intermingle and melt into one another, but nevertheless in the ordinary man they have a tendency to lie in more or less regular bands, while the outline of the body becomes fairly definite and regular. With our savage, however, all is ill-regulated and confused; he is obviously a creature of violent and often vicious impulses to which he instantly yields without the slightest effort to control them. A very unpleasant person altogether; yet every one of us has passed through this stage, and by the experience gained in it we have been enabled to rise out of it to something purer and nobler.

Only some of the lower negro races and the relics of the third root-race now represent a stage of evolution as early as this. Many of those whom we call savages (as, for example, some among the Zulus, the Maoris, or the South Sea Islanders) are already considerably developed, and would compare favourably with the lower specimens of our own civilization. The astral bodies of these comparatively superior savages are usually intermediates between Plate X. and Plate VII., though naturally there is a wide range of individual variation.

It will be very necessary for us to bear constantly in mind, in our endeavour to realise the appearance of the various vehicles, that the particles of which they are composed are always in rapid motion. In certain cases, which will be specially mentioned in their turn, there are definite bands and clearly defined lines in these bodies; but in the vast majority the clouds of colour not only melt into one another, but are all the while rolling over one another, and appearing and disappearing as they roll. Indeed the surface of this luminous and brightly-coloured mist resembles somewhat the surface of violently boiling water in the way in which the particles are seen to swirl about, to rise to the surface and sink back again, and constantly to change places with one another. So that the various colours by no means retain always the respective positions in which they are represented in our illustrations. Yet it is nevertheless true that they gravitate towards the arrangement indicated —that though the yellow, the rose and the blue are not always to be found grouped exactly as depicted, yet in all their whirlings and rollings they remain near the upper part of the oval; they are always to be found near the head of the physical body, when they exist at all, while the colours indicating selfishness, avarice, deceit or hatred tend always towards the bottom, and the great mass of sensual feeling floats usually between the two.

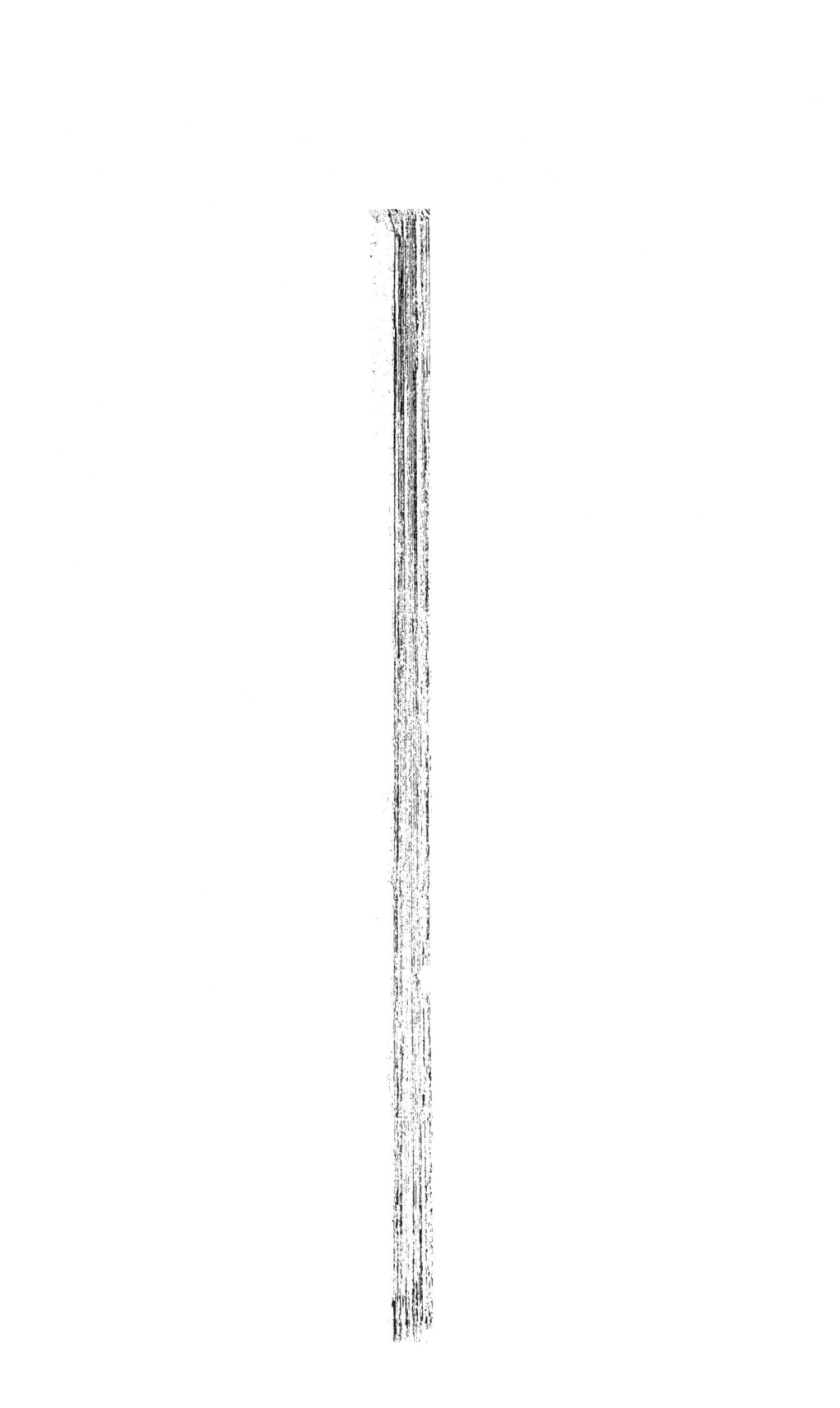

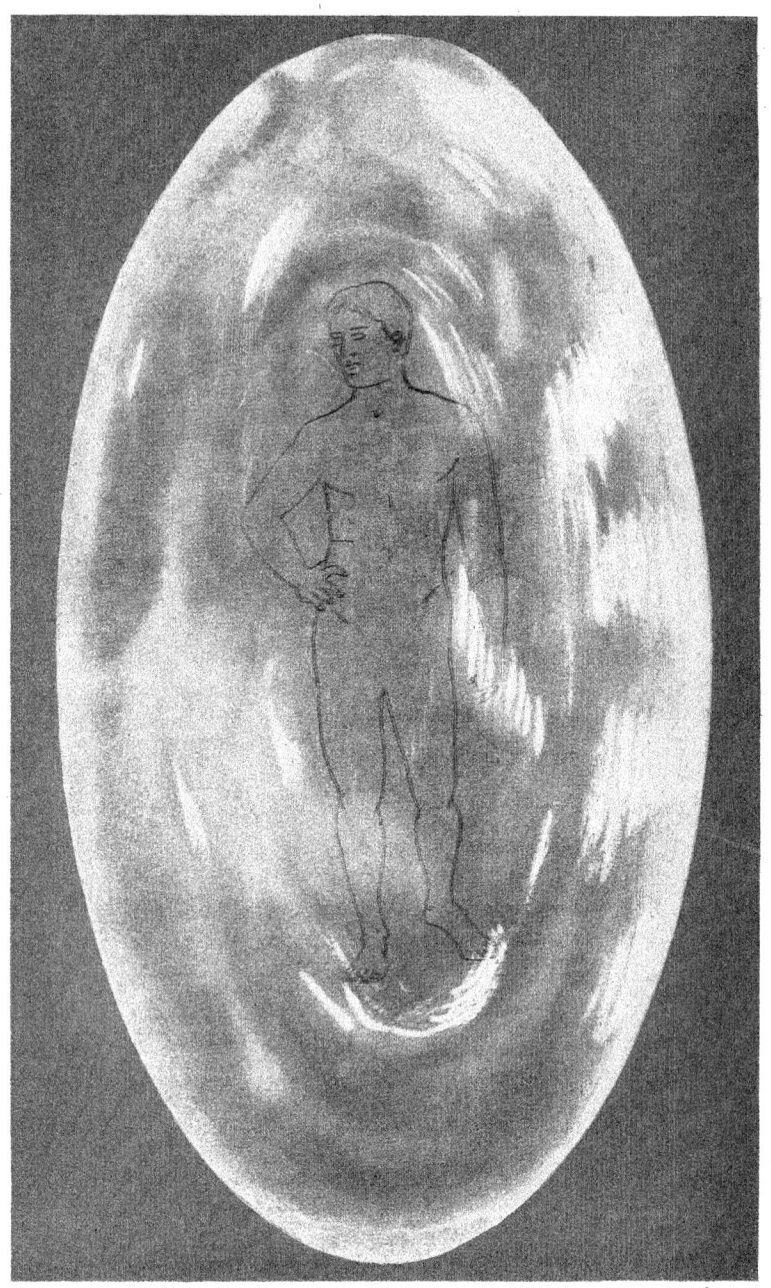

Photochromogravure, Lyons & London

VIII

Each of these rates of vibration (which show themselves to us as colour) has its own special type of astral matter upon which it can operate most freely, so the average position of these colours in the corresponding vibration depends in reality upon the respective specific gravity of its special matter. The whole, or almost the whole, of the matter in an astral body may be temporarily forced by a sudden rush of passion to vibrate at a certain rate, but all of it except that to which the vibration is natural will fall back into its ordinary rate when the force is removed.

Naturally each man has his individual idiosyncrasies, and no two are exactly alike, but each illustration given represents a section of an average specimen of its class, and the various colours are shown in that part of the body where they are usually to be found. The outline of the physical body is faintly marked, and each mist cloud merely to help to give the reader the conception of the thing in comparison with that of the physical man that he knows; indeed in this respect there is less to be said until we come to consider the higher principles later, when we find that a vast change greatly increases in density thereafter.

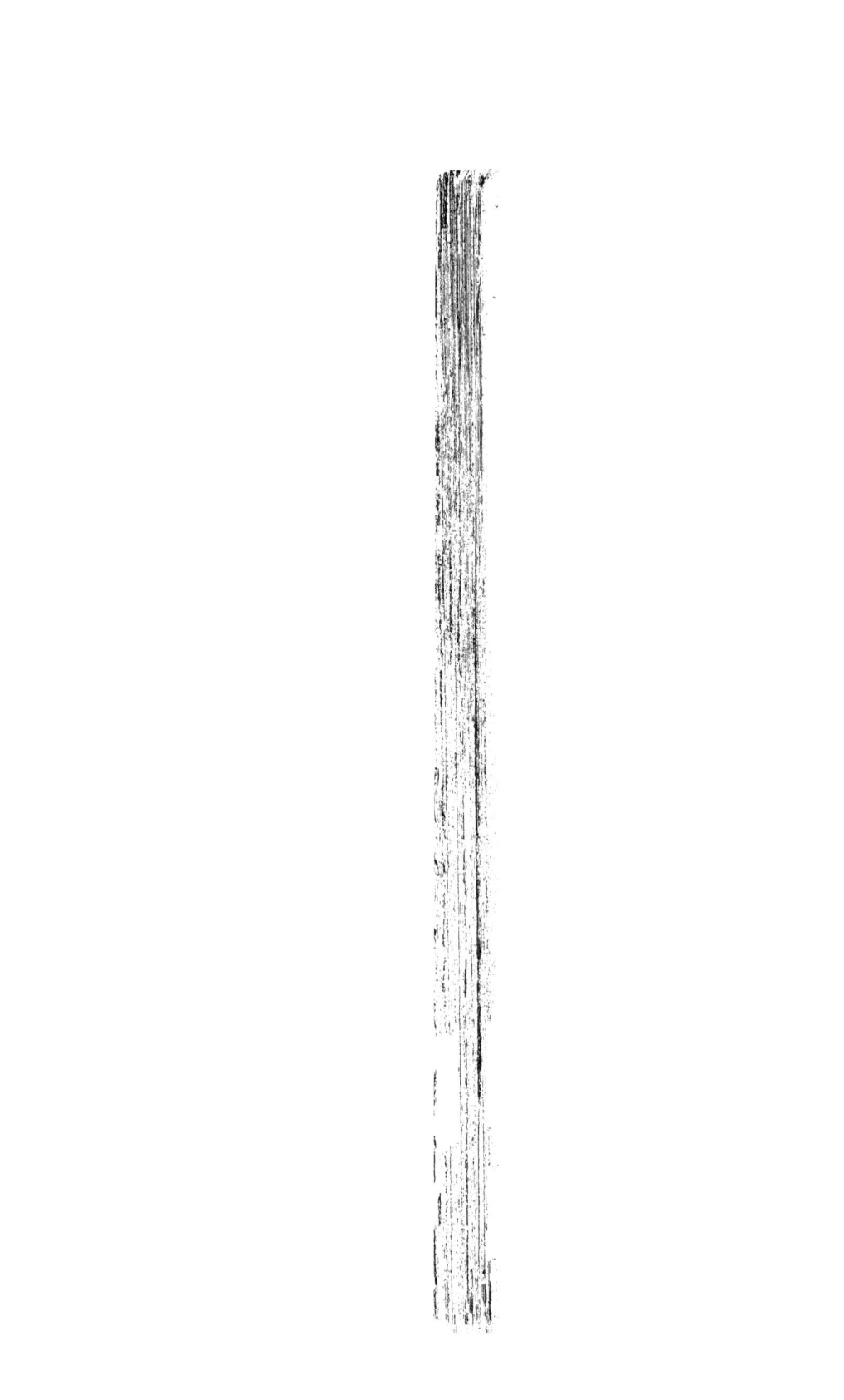

Each of these rates of vibration (which show themselves to us as colours) has its own special type of astral or mental matter in which it can operate most freely, and the average position of these colours in the ever-shifting mist-cloud depends in reality upon the respective specific gravity of its special matter. The whole, or almost the whole, of the matter in an astral body may be temporarily forced by a sudden rush of passion to vibrate at a certain rate; but all of it except that to which the vibration is natural will fall back into its ordinary rate when the force is removed.

Naturally each man has his individual idiosyncrasies, and no two are exactly alike; but each illustration given represents a section of an average specimen of its class, and its various colours are shown in that part of the ovoid where they are usually to be found. The outline of the physical body is faintly marked inside each mist-cloud merely to keep clearly before the reader the conception of its size in comparison with that of those higher vehicles: though indeed in this respect there is but little variation until we come to consider the highly developed man, when we find that the finer vehicles greatly increase in size, as will be shown hereafter.

Chapter XV

THE ORDINARY PERSON

Let us now turn from the consideration of the savage to examine the ordinary average "man in the street" of our own race and period, in order that we may see what advancement has been made, and in what way it shows itself in the various vehicles. For our example we will not take the student, or the highly cultured and refined person; but simply the ordinary lower middle-class man—the small grocer, or clerk, the concierge, the postman—not the roughest sort of man, but simply the ordinary average—the "commonplace type with a stick and a pipe," so well described in *Patience*. Looking with appropriate sight at the causal body of such a man, we shall find it at about the degree of development indicated in Plate VIII. It will be seen that there has been a distinct increase in the content of the great ovoid film; a certain amount of exceedingly delicate and ethereal colour now exists within it, though it is still less than half filled. The general meaning of the colours is the

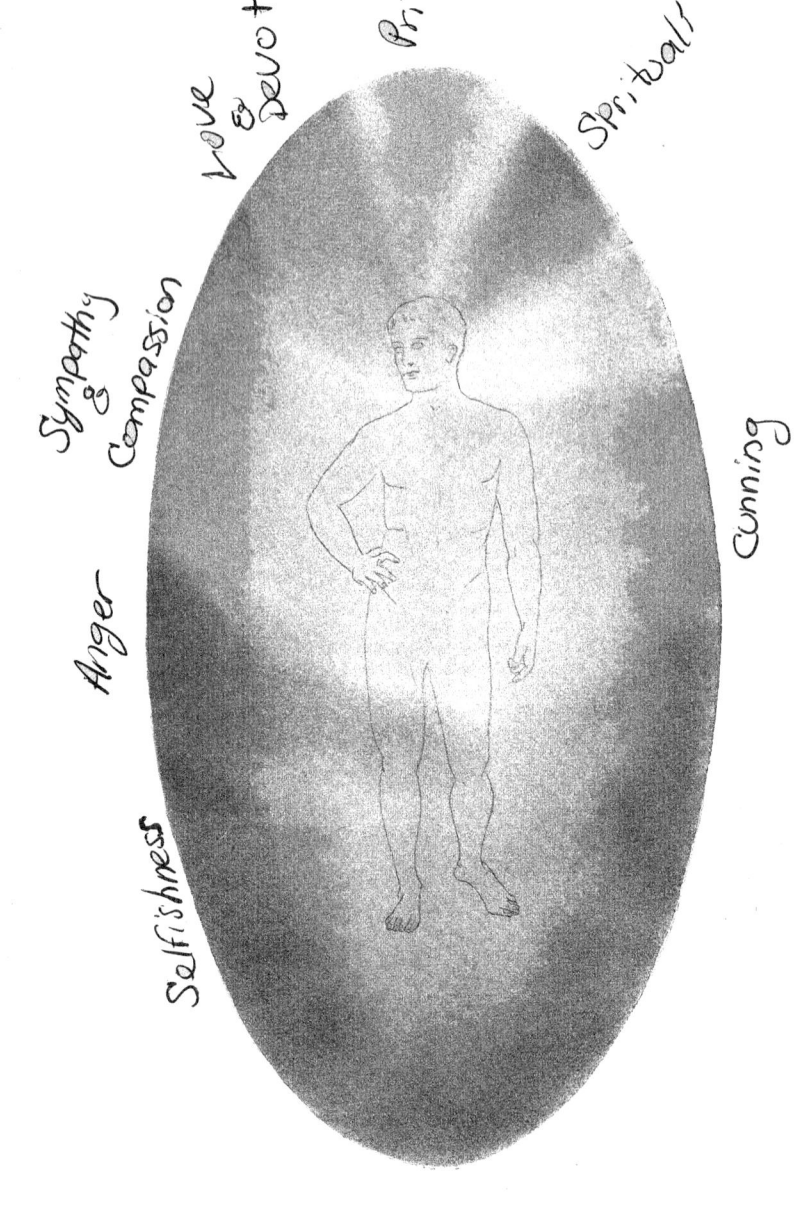

same as at lower levels, although here they indicate qualities definitely and permanently acquired by the soul, and they are many octaves higher than the colours which represent the same qualities on inferior planes. It will be seen that something of the higher intellect, something of the power of true devotion and true unselfish love, has already been developed within the man; and whatever expression of this may be possible upon the lower planes will be his as a kind of stock-in-trade or inherent quality in every incarnation which the future holds in store for him. There is even already a faint tint of that exceedingly delicate violet which indicates the capacity of love and devotion turned towards the highest ideal, and also a faint hint of the clear green of sympathy and compassion.

Examining the mental body of the ordinary man as pictured in Plate IX., we find that it already shows considerable improvement upon that of the savage. It is not only that there is more in proportion of intellect, love and devotion; but that all of these characteristics have improved very greatly in their quality. Though very far yet from being perfectly pure, they are yet certainly far better in tone than those in Plate VI. The proportion of pride is quite as high as before, but at least it is now pride at a higher level; if the man is still proud, it will be rather

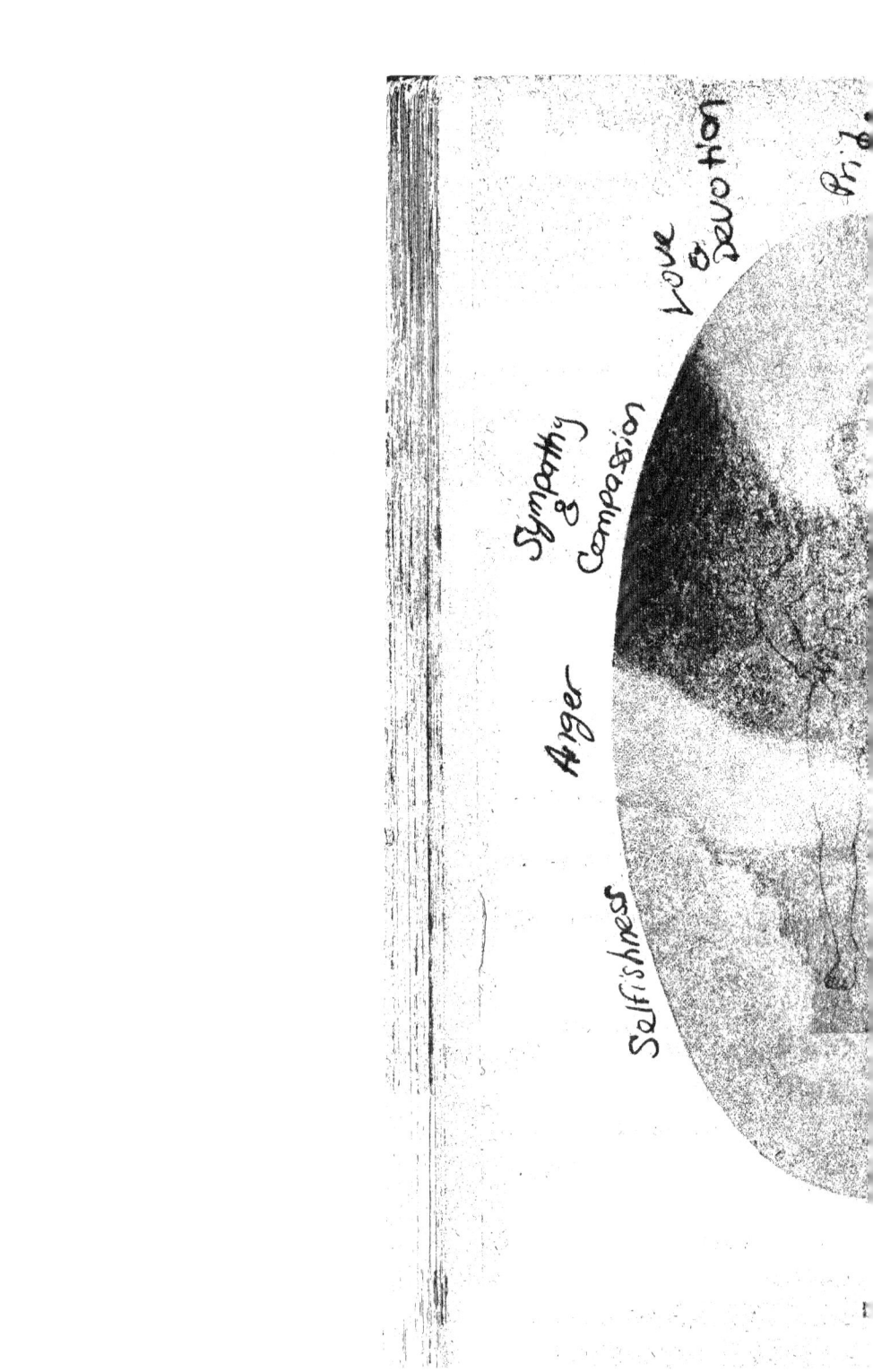

same as at lower levels, although here they indicate qualities definitely and permanently acquired by the soul, and they are many octaves higher than the colours which represent the same qualities on inferior planes. It will be seen that something of the higher intellect, something of the power of true devotion and true unselfish love, has already been developed within the man; and whatever expression of this may be possible upon the lower planes will be his as a kind of stock-in-trade or inherent quality in every incarnation which the future holds in store for him. There is even already a faint tint of that exceedingly delicate violet which indicates the capacity of love and devotion turned towards the highest ideal, and also a faint hint of the clear green of sympathy and compassion.

Examining the mental body of the ordinary man as pictured in Plate IX., we find that it already shows considerable improvement upon that of the savage. It is not only that there is more in proportion of intellect, love and devotion; but that all of these characteristics have improved very greatly in their quality. Though very far yet from being perfectly pure, they are yet certainly far better in tone than those in Plate VI. The proportion of pride is quite as high as before, but at least it is now pride at a higher level; if the man is still proud, it will be rather of such good qualities as he imagines himself to possess than merely of physical pre-eminence in brute force or in cruelty. There is still a good deal of the scarlet which indicates liability to anger, but it is noticeable that it now takes a much lower place in the cloud, which indicates an improvement in the general quality of the matter of which this mind-body is composed. The low type of green in the mental body of the savage (which indicates deceit very strongly tinged by avarice and selfishness) required for its vibrations a type of matter denser and coarser than that needed by the scarlet of anger. The decidedly better green which shows in the mental body of the ordinary man needs for its vibration matter of a type somewhat less dense than the scarlet; and hence apparently the change of relative position. The green has now advanced to the indication of a certain amount of versatility and adaptability, rather than deceit or cunning. A large proportion of the mind is still occupied by the brown of selfish tendencies; but even this colour will be seen to be a trifle warmer and less grim than before.

If we now turn to Plate X. we shall find the astral body which corresponds to the mental body in Plate IX.—the astral body of the ordinary man. It will be seen that this astral body agrees very closely with its mental, though its colours are naturally somewhat coarser and it contains very decided indications of certain passions which cannot be expressed on the higher plane. Still it will be found very much improved as compared with the astral body of the savage on Plate VII. There is less of sensuality, though that is still unfortunately one of the most prominent characteristics; but at least it is less utterly brutal and overpowering than it was. Selfishness is still very prominent, and the capability of deceit for personal ends is still undoubtedly present; but already the green seems to be dividing itself into two distinct qualities, showing that mere cunning is gradually becoming adaptability.

This drawing of the astral body represents not only the average quality of that of the type of man to which it belongs, but also its average condition when comparatively at rest. The astral body of any ordinary person is so very rarely at rest that we should gain but a very incomplete idea of the possibilities of its appearance if we omitted to consider it as it is when affected by sudden impulses or rushes of feeling. There are also certain more permanent attitudes of mind which produce modifications of the astral body that are sufficiently distinctive to be worthy of remark, and we shall now devote a few plates to illustrating these various affects.

Chapter XVI

SUDDEN EMOTIONS

Some of these produce most striking results in the astral body—results which are well worth careful study. For instance, by turning to Plate XI., we shall see an attempt to picture the effect which is visible when a sudden wave of strong and perfectly pure affection sweeps over a person —when, for example, a mother snatches up her baby and covers it with kisses. In a moment the astral body is thrown into violent agitation, and the original colours are for the time almost obscured. In this, as in all these cases, the astral body of the ordinary person, as given in Plate X., is taken as a basis or back-ground, though during the passage of the violent emotion, but little is seen of it. If the change introduced in Plate XI. is analysed it will be found to consist of four separate parts. Certain coils or vortices of vivid colour are to be seen, well-defined and solid-looking, and glowing with an intense light from within. Each of these is

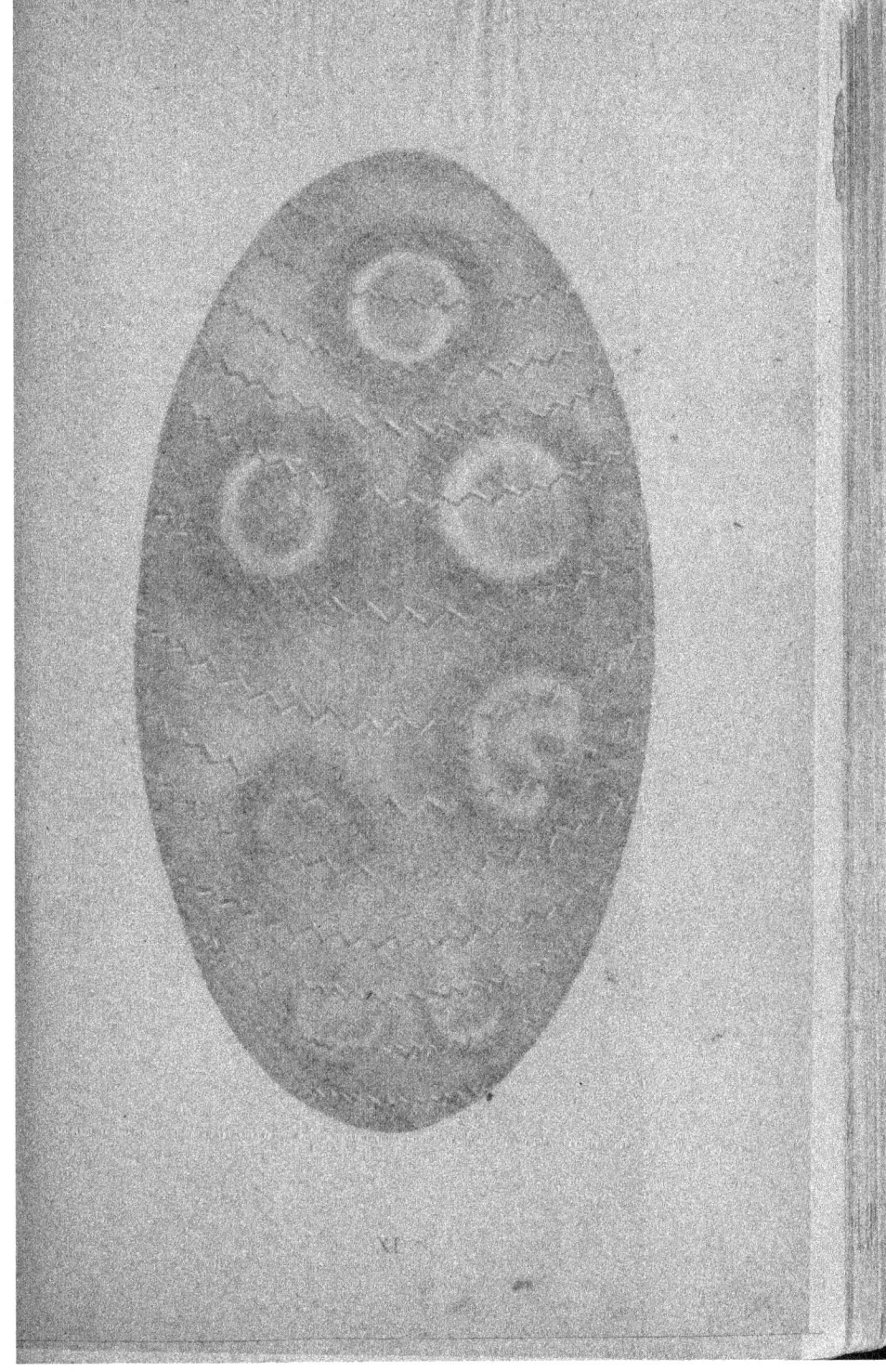

Chapter XVI

SUDDEN EMOTIONS

Some of these produce most striking results in the astral body—results which are well worth careful study. For instance, by turning to Plate XI., we shall see an attempt to picture the effect which is visible when a sudden wave of strong and perfectly pure affection sweeps over a person —when, for example, a mother snatches up her baby and covers it with kisses. In a moment the astral body is thrown into violent agitation, and the original colours are for the time almost obscured. In this, as in all these cases, the astral body of the ordinary person, as given in Plate X., is taken as a basis or back-ground, though during the passage of the violent emotion, but little is seen of it. If the change introduced in Plate XI. is analysed it will be found to consist of four separate parts. Certain coils or vortices of vivid colour are to be seen, well-defined and solid-looking, and glowing with an intense light from within. Each of these is

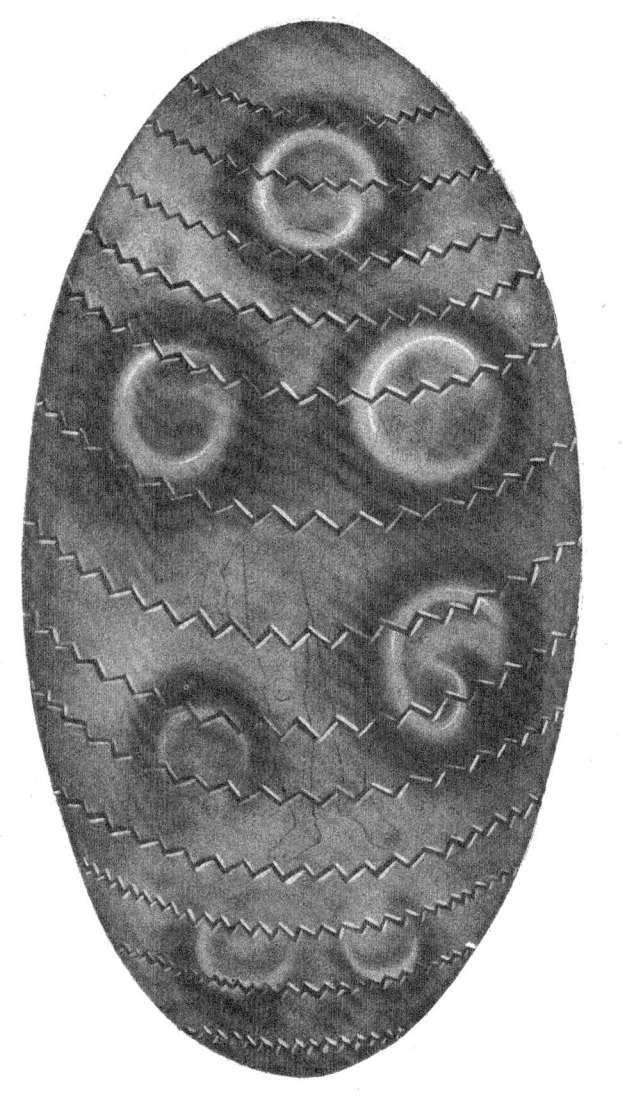

XI

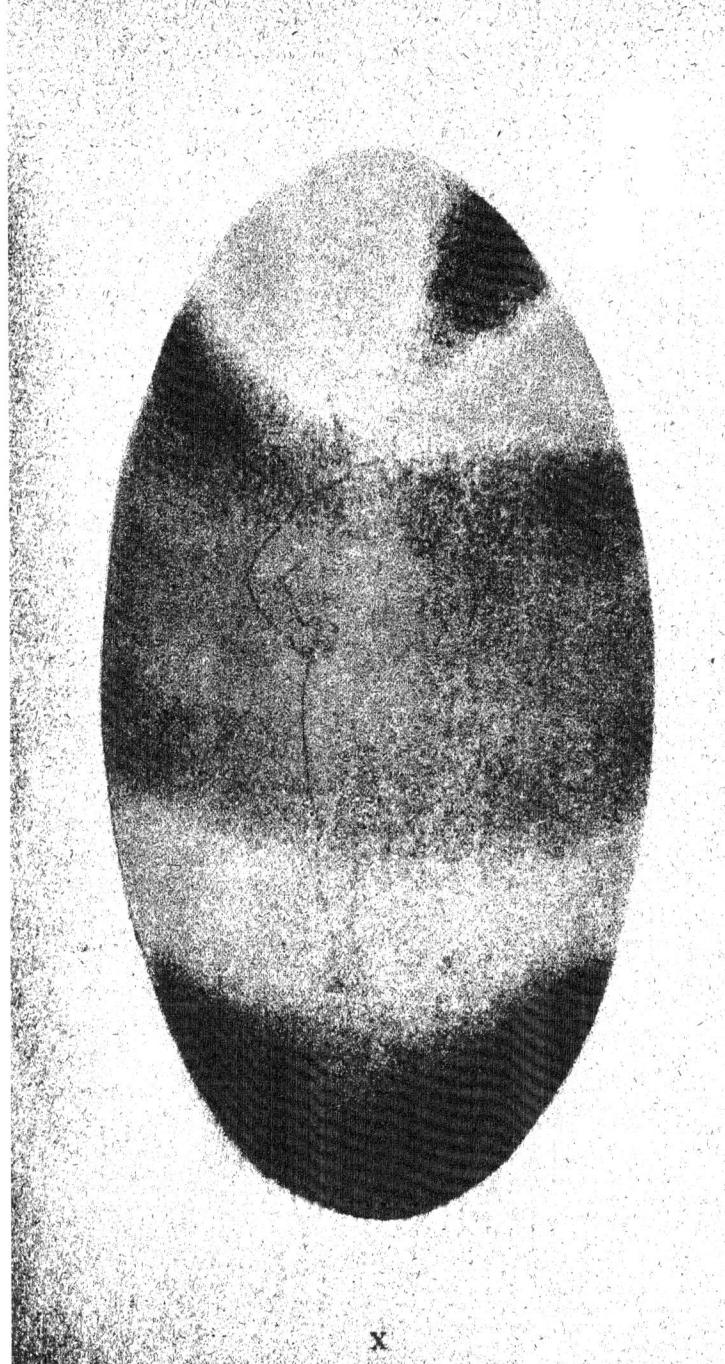

x

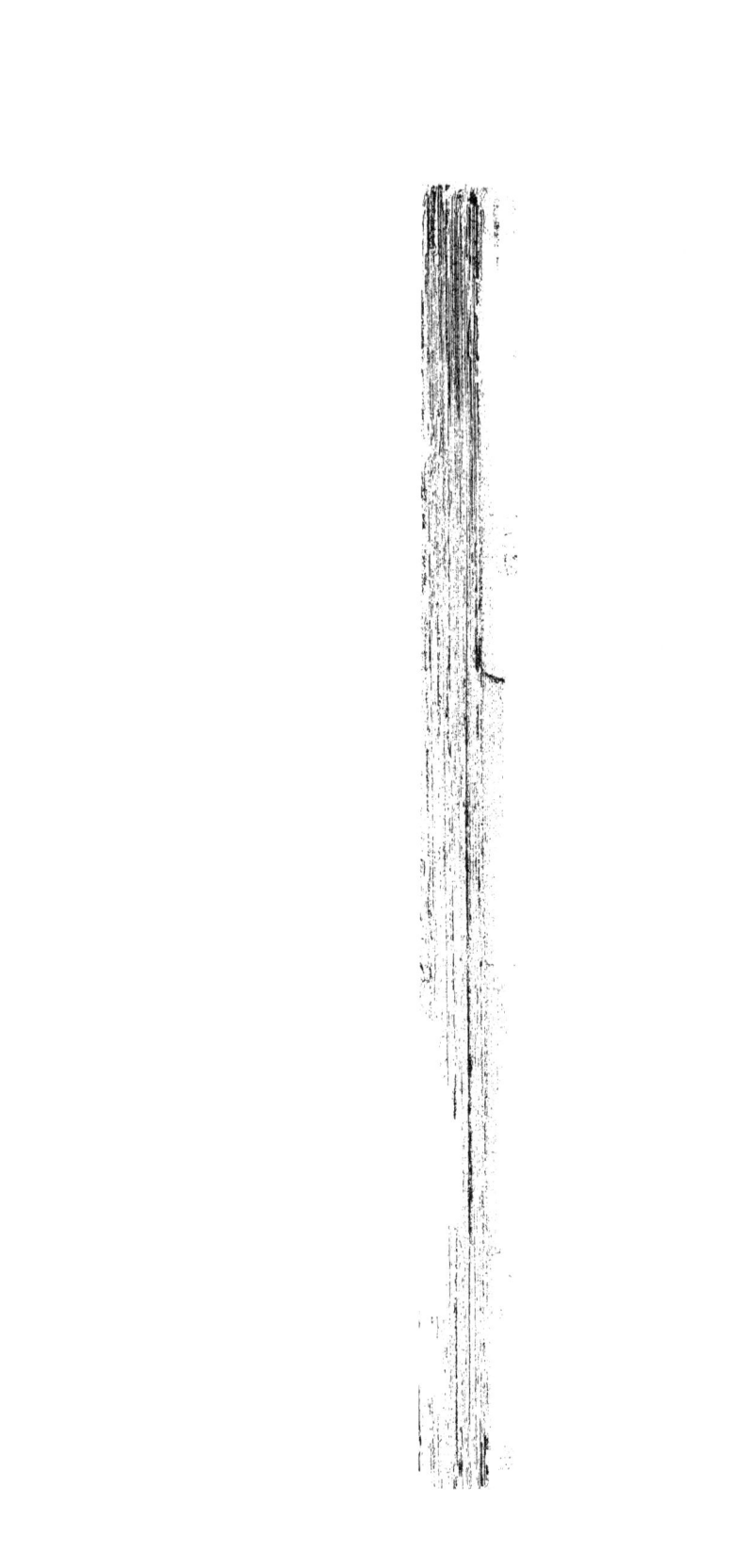

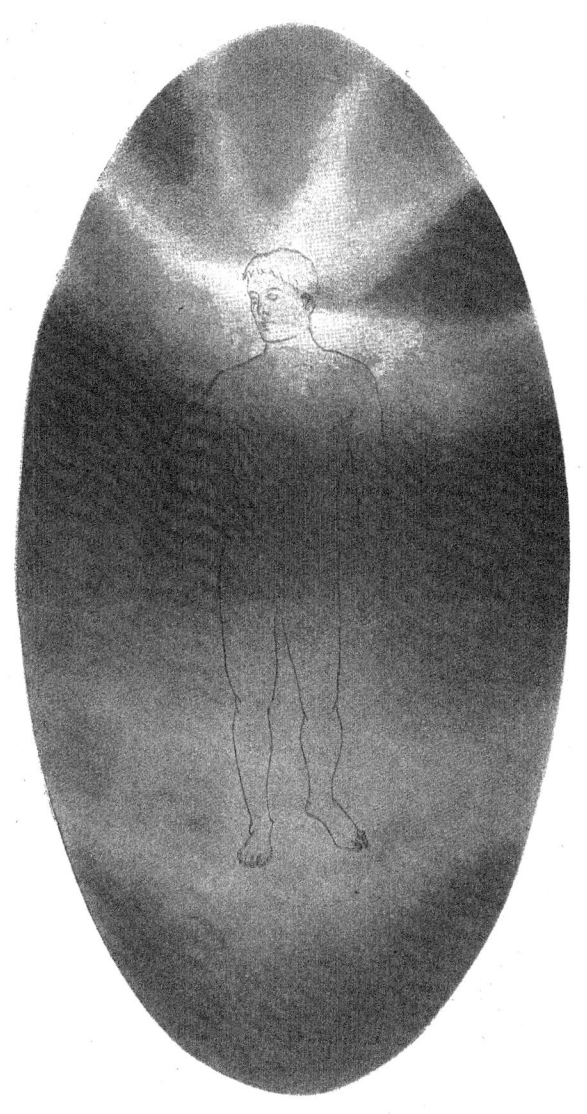

X

in reality a thought-form of intense affection, generated within the astral body, and about to be poured forth from it towards the object of the feeling. It is difficult to depict these whirling clouds of living light, but their real appearance is indescribably lovely.

2. The whole astral body is crossed by horizontal pulsating lines of crimson light, more difficult to represent accurately even than the thought-forms, by reason of the exceeding rapidity of their motion. The general effect, however, has been very happily caught by the artist.

3. A kind of film of rose-colour covers the surface of the whole astral body, so that all within is seen through it, as through tinted glass. In the drawing this shows only at the edges.

4. A sort of crimson flush filling the entire astral body, tinging to some extent all the other hues, and here and there condensing itself into irregular floating wisps, like half-formed cirrus clouds.

This magnificent display of astral fireworks would probably last only a few seconds, and then the body would rapidly resume its normal condition. Yet every such rush of feeling produces its effect; it adds a little to the crimson in the higher part of the oval, and it makes it a little easier for the particles of the astral body to respond to the next wave of affection which comes. Transient though such an impulse may be, yet as it occurs again and again its effects are cumulative; and another point which must not be forgotten is the good influence upon others which is produced by the radiation of vivid vibrations of love and joy.

Devotion

Except that blue is everywhere substituted for crimson, Plate XII. is almost identical with Plate XI. It illustrates a sudden accession of devotional impulse which surged over a nun while engaged in contemplation. All the four forms of manifestation which we noted in connection with the impulse of affection are also observable here—the whirling, gleaming coils, the rapidly-vibrating horizontal lines, the outer film and the wisps of cloud — and their signification is precisely the same, substituting everywhere religious feeling for affection.

So perfect an outburst of devotion is somewhat rare—much less common than a similarly perfect outburst of love. A rush of feeling of this nature, but generally without its definiteness or precision, may sometimes be seen to occur in the case of one who offers an act of adoration before an altar, or perhaps a picture of the Blessed

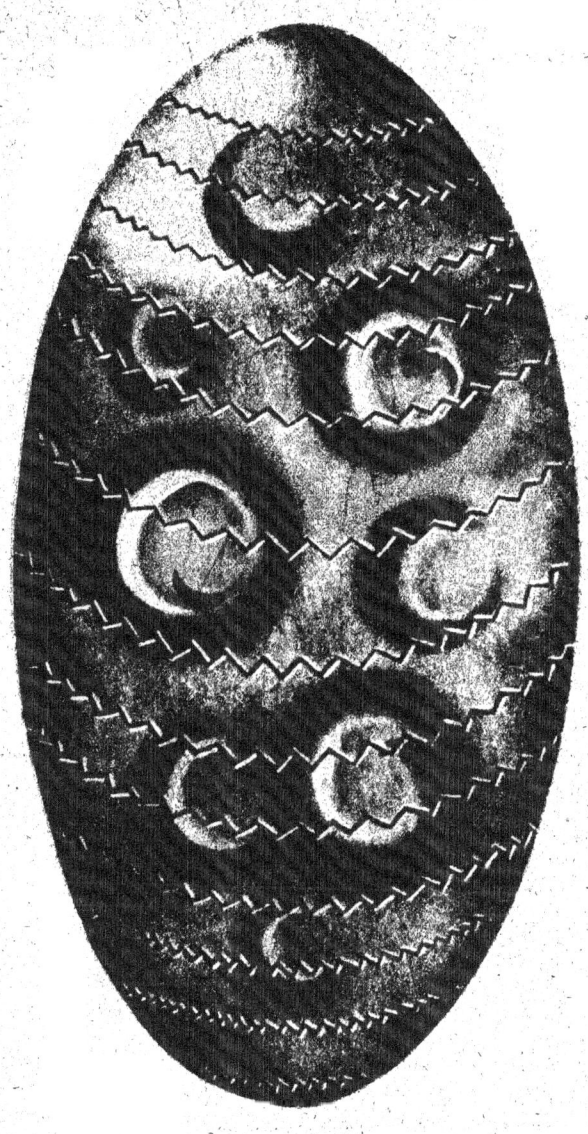

XII

little easier for the particles of the astral body to respond to the next wave of affection which comes. Transient though such an impulse may be, yet as it occurs again and again its effects are cumulative; and another point which must not be forgotten, is the good influence upon others which is produced by the radiation of vivid vibrations of love and joy.

... ... were substituted ... ... almost identical with ... ... a sudden accession of ... ... impulse which surged ... ... a man while engaged in contemplation. All the four forms of manifestation which we noted in connection with the impulse of affection are also observable here—the whirling, gleaming coils, the rapidly vibrating horizontal lines, the outer film and the wisps of cloud — and their signification is precisely the same, substituting everywhere religious feeling for affection.

So perfect an outburst of devotion is somewhat rare—much less common than a similarly perfect outburst of love. A rush of feeling of this nature, but generally without its definiteness or precision, may sometimes be seen to occur in the case of one who offers an act of adoration before an altar, or perhaps a picture of the Blessed

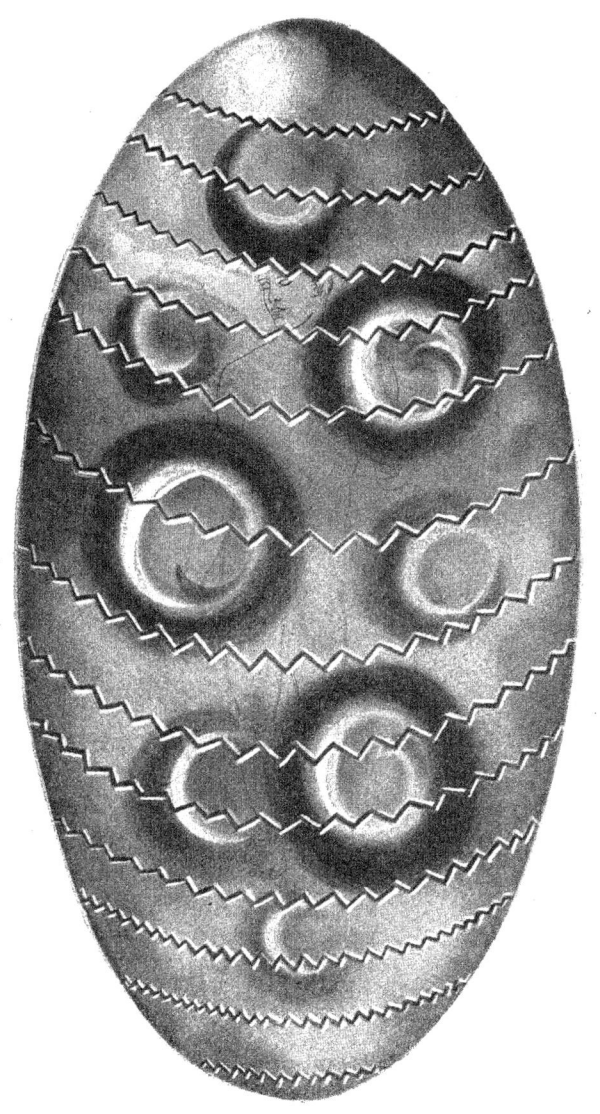

XII

Virgin. Usually the parallel lines would be less regular and less prominent, and the sharply defined coils would be altogether absent, their place being taken by shapeless clouds of blue vapour.

Quite often such shapeless clouds of heavy blue may be seen rolling slowly along like wreaths of dense smoke over the heads of the congregation of a church. But this is not at all observable in the ordinary fashionable church, where the minds of the men are working over again the vicissitudes of their latest speculation, and the ladies are deeply absorbed in the delights of criticising each other's millinery; nor does it ever show itself in those dour "protestant" conventicles, where there is no thought of anything so humble as worship or devotion, but only conceit and self-righteousness, alike in the stilted and pompous oration of the speaker, and in the smug disputatious heresy-hunting attitude of the hearers. But occasionally as an accompaniment to the heartfelt though unmusical singing among illiterate dissenters, or sometimes among the poor peasants in a Catholic church, or more often still at the hearty and earnest service of what is called a ritualistic church, a great deal of very real devotion manifests itself in this way. It is not perhaps especially intelligent, for the great blue clouds are rarely lit by even the faintest gleam of gold; but at least it is genuine as far as it goes, and it has undoubtedly an elevating effect upon those by whom it is felt.

In the great majority of cases, however, devotion as a sentiment seems to be vague and ill-defined, and so fine a specimen as that given in our illustration is indeed rare.

Intense Anger

Plate XIII. is perhaps the most striking in appearance of the whole series, and even without any explanation it would of itself be an eloquent warning against the folly and wickedness of yielding to a fit of passion. As in the previous cases, the ordinary background of the astral body is temporarily obscured by the rush of feeling, but now the strong and vivid thoughts are unfortunately those of malice and ill-will. They express themselves once more as coils or vortices, but this time as heavy, thunderous masses of sooty blackness, lit up from within by the lurid glow of active hatred. Less defined wisps of the same dark cloud are to be seen defiling the whole astral body, while the fiery arrows of uncontrolled anger shoot among them like flashes of lightning. A tremendous and truly awful spectacle; and the more fully it is understood the more terrible it appears. For this is the case of a man who is absolutely transported and

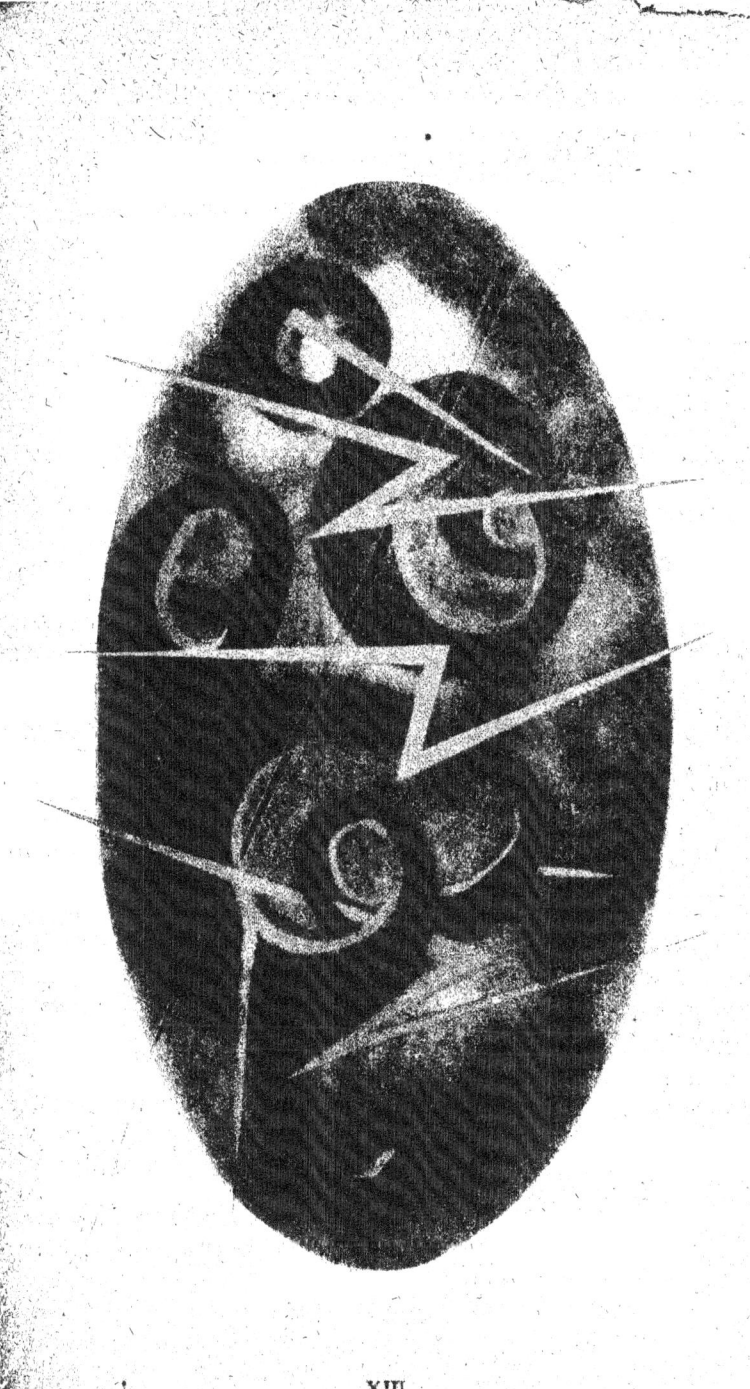

XIII

faintest gleam of gold; but at least it is genuine as far as it goes, and it has undoubtedly an elevating effect upon those by whom it is felt.

In the great majority of cases, however, devotion as a sentiment seems to be vague and ill-defined, and so fine a specimen as that given in our illustration is indeed rare.

Intense Anger

Plate XIII. is perhaps the most striking in appearance of the whole series, and even without any explanation it would of itself be an eloquent warning against the folly and wickedness of yielding to a fit of passion. As in the previous cases, the ordinary background of the astral body is temporarily obscured by the rush of feeling, but now the strong and vivid thoughts are unfortunately those of malice and ill-will. They express themselves once more as coils or vortices, but this time as heavy, thunderous masses of sooty blackness, lit up from within by the lurid glow of active hatred. Less defined wisps of the same dark cloud are to be seen defiling the whole astral body, while the fiery arrows of uncontrolled anger shoot among them like flashes of lightning. A tremendous and truly awful spectacle; and the more fully it is understood the more terrible it appears. For this is the case of a man who is absolutely transported and

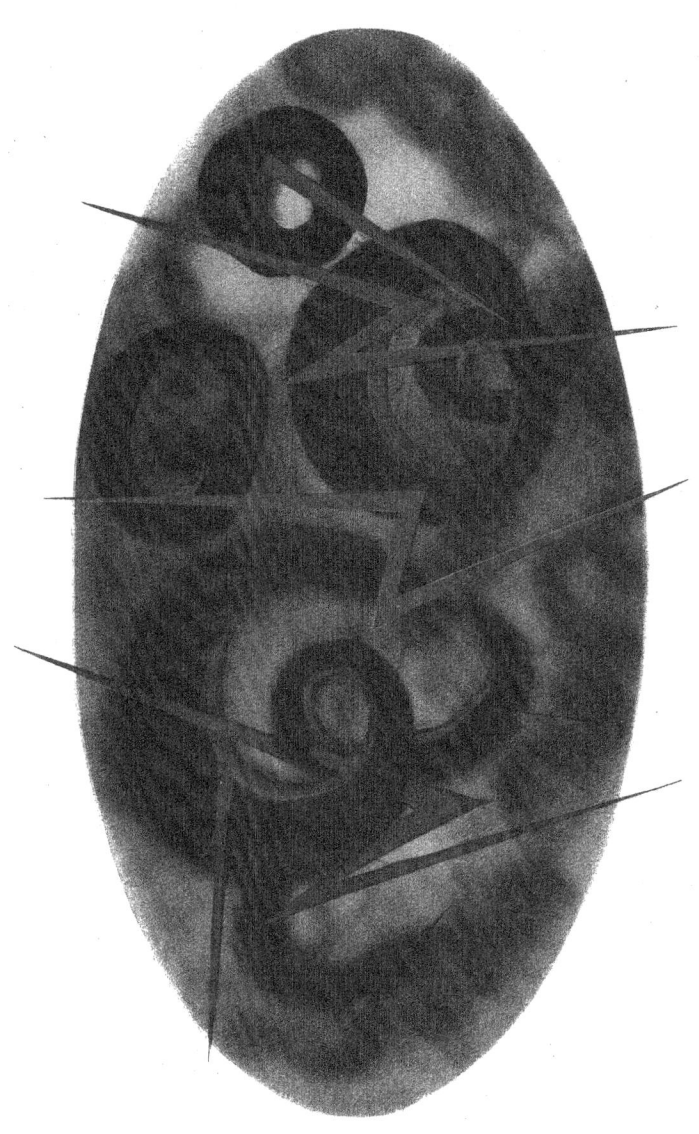

XIII

beside himself with rage—a man who for the time being has utterly lost control of himself, and is capable of murder or of the most atrocious cruelties. He may be hurried into the commission of any crime, and in one moment may commit an action for which a whole life of repentance can never atone. Even should the discipline of education and custom still withhold him from outward violence, those terrible flashes are penetrating other astral bodies like swords, and the man is injuring those about him just as really as, though less visibly than, if he assaulted them on the physical plane.

An additional horror is imported by the consideration that while he is thus a source of danger to others, he is utterly defenceless himself. For the moment passion has entirely controlled him; the desire-elemental is supreme, and the true man has temporarily lost hold of his vehicle. Under those circumstances another and stronger will may seize that which he has allowed to be wrested from him. Another entity, watching and waiting, may as it were grasp the rudder of the momentarily abandoned craft, and hold possession against the true captain on his return. In other words, at such a moment, when a man is transported with rage, he is liable to be seized and obsessed either by a dead man of similar nature or by some evil artificial elemental whose vibrations synchronize with those which are dominating him. Not only is he a danger to his fellows, but he is in appalling danger himself.

The case selected for illustration is of course an extreme one, and such a condition would not usually last more than a few minutes. But every one who falls into a passion exhibits these characteristics to some extent; and one cannot but feel that if men only knew how they appeared in the eyes of those who can see, when they yield themselves to these outbursts of anger, they would surely take far greater care to avoid them.

The gust of passion passes away, but it leaves its mark behind. In the astral body of the average man there is always a certain amount of scarlet, which indicates the capacity for anger, the possibility of being irritated; and each outburst of rage would add something to this, and would predispose the matter of the entire vehicle to respond somewhat more readily than before to these very undesirable vibrations.

It may also be remembered that though the passion may be impermanent, the record of it remains for ever in the memory of nature; though the elemental created by an evil wish will cease to exist after a period proportioned to the strength of that wish, yet the living

XIV

photograph of every scene … … …
and all the widespreading … … …
during that life are charged with … … …
to the karma of … … …

… … …

The … of fear upon the astral body is very
stri[king]. … sudden shock of terror will in an
in[stant suffuse] the whole body with a curious
livid grey mist, while horizontal lines of the same
hue appear, but vibrate with such violence as to
be hardly recognisable as separate lines. The
result is indescribably ghastly, and it is impossible
to convey an adequate idea of it by illustration.
Plate XIV. gives such suggestion of it as can
be put upon paper, but it can hardly depict
the strange way in which all light fades away for
the time from the body, and the whole grey mass
quivers helplessly like a jelly.

Such an appearance as this … … …
panic, and … … would soon … …
A condition of permanent fear or extreme
nervousness will express itself in a milder sort
form of the same phenomena, … … …
tinge of grey and the characteristic … …
irregular lines of this haunting emotion.

photograph of every instant of its life remains, and all the wide-spreading results of its actions during that life are charged with absolute justice to the karma of its creator.

Fear

The effect of fear upon the astral body is very striking. A sudden shock of terror will in an instant suffuse the whole body with a curious livid grey mist, while horizontal lines of the same hue appear, but vibrate with such violence as to be hardly recognisable as separate lines. The result is indescribably ghastly, and it is impossible to convey an adequate idea of it by illustration. Plate XIV. gives such suggestion of it as can be put upon paper, but it can hardly depict the strange way in which all light fades out for the time from the body, and the whole grey mass quivers helplessly like a jelly.

Such an appearance as this denotes deadly panic, and ordinarily would soon pass away. A condition of permanent fear or extreme nervousness will express itself in a much modified form of the same phenomena, but the peculiar tinge of grey, and the characteristic quiver, are invariable signs of this haunting presence.

Chapter XVII

MORE PERMANENT CONDITIONS

WE have endeavoured to illustrate the immediate effect of some of the sudden emotions which affect the outer vehicles of man, and to explain that, quickly as they pass, they are not without permanent results to the soul within. It remains for us to describe the way in which certain dispositions or types of character manifest themselves, so that it may be seen to what extent each of these modifies the progress of the man upon his upward path.

There is one influence, however, which produces a considerable result in the lives of most men, which does not exactly belong to either of these categories. It is often sudden in its advent, and in most cases it is certainly not lifelong in its duration; but still it does not fade away so rapidly as those which we have been considering. Nevertheless, in the life of such a man as is imaged in Plates VIII., IX., and X. it is usually the main event; indeed it is very frequently the one really bright spot in an existence which is otherwise monotonous, sordid and selfish—the only occasion on which such a personality is lifted temporarily out of himself, and lives for awhile on an altogether higher level.

This sudden elevation comes to the person who, as it is commonly called, "falls in love." It is difficult for those of us who are so happy as to live the wider and more cultured life to realise how tremendous is the temporary change which this "falling in love" brings into the existence of the less developed man whom we have been describing as ordinary. Those who live in the freer atmosphere of art and music, of science and philosophy, of world-wide interests and habitually altruistic thought, find it difficult to put themselves back in imagination into the condition of evolution through which they passed ages ago—the condition of the less developed soul, with its intense self-centredness, its strangely limited horizon, its indescribably petty and sordid outlook. Assuredly within these younger souls also the divine lies latent, and when occasion offers it will not infrequently shine forth in deeds of splendid heroism and of magnificent self-sacrifice. Yet this undoubted possibility does not alter the fact that such souls *are* younger, and that under ordinary circumstances they live the less-developed life of which we have spoken.

Into a life thus cramped and limited there suddenly shines a gleam from above, and the divine spark within glows brighter in response. Later, the man may lose it again, and descend once more into the murky light of common day; yet nothing can take away from him the experience that for him also once the golden gates have opened, and the glory of the higher life has been to some extent revealed. He has at least passed through a phase when for a longer or shorter period self was dethroned, and another entity occupied the first place in his world; and thus he learns, for the first time, one of the most valuable lessons in the whole course of his evolution. It will be æons yet before that lesson is perfectly assimilated, yet even this first glimpse of it is of enormous importance to the ego, and its effect on the astral body is worthy of special notice.

The transformation is unexpected and complete, as will be seen by comparing Plate X. with Plate XV. The two bodies could not be recognised as belonging to the same person, so extraordinary is the alteration. It will be seen that certain qualities have altogether disappeared for the time, that others have been enormously increased, and that their relative positions have considerably changed.

Selfishness, deceit and avarice have vanished,

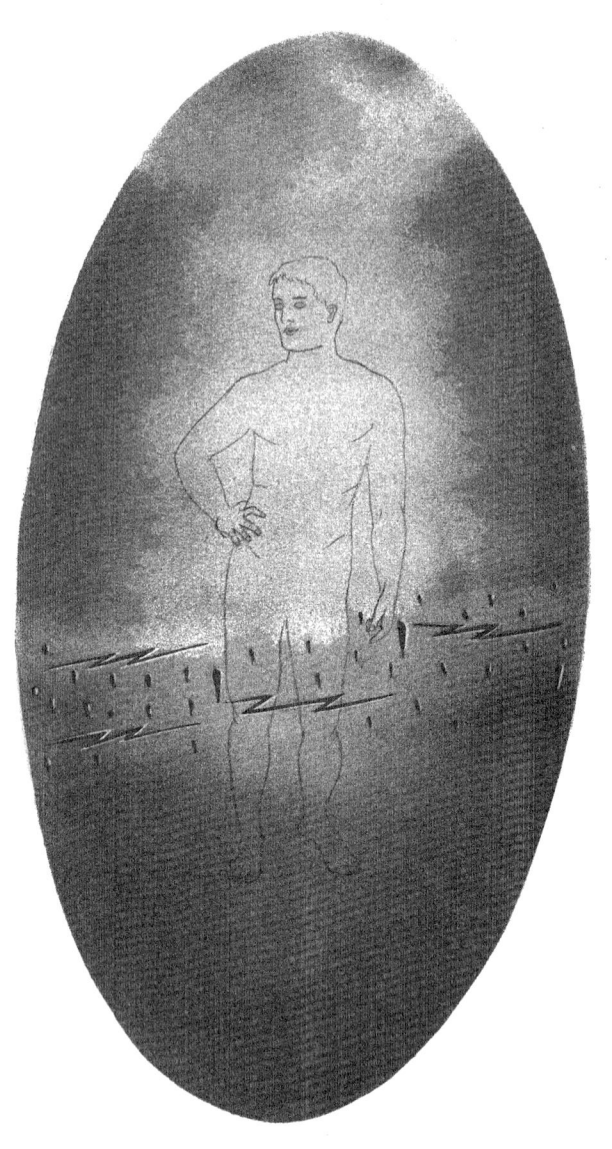

XV

and the lowest part of the oval is now filled with a large development of animal passions. The green of adaptability has been replaced by the peculiar brownish-green of jealousy, and the extreme activity of this feeling is shown by the bright scarlet flashes of anger which permeate it.

But the undesirable changes are more than counterbalanced by the splendid band of crimson which fills so large a part of the oval. This is for the time a dominant characteristic, and the whole astral body glows with its light. Under its influence the general muddiness of the ordinary body has disappeared, and the hues are all brilliant and clearly marked, good and bad alike. It is an intensification of the life in various directions.

It will be noticed that the blue of devotion is also distinctly improved, and even (so much has the nature been temporarily elevated) a touch of pale violet appears at the summit of the ovoid, indicating a capacity of response to a really high and unselfish ideal. The yellow of intellect, however, has entirely vanished for the time—which I suppose would be considered by the cynical as characteristic of the condition!

It seems scarcely possible that after all this brilliant development the man should sink back

and the lowest part of the oval is now filled with a large development of animal passions. The green of adaptability has been replaced by the peculiar brownish-green of jealousy, and the extreme activity of this feeling is shown by the bright scarlet flashes of anger which permeate it.

But the undesirable changes are more than counterbalanced by the splendid band of crimson which fills so large a part of the oval. This is for the time a dominant characteristic, and the whole astral body glows with its light. Under its influence the general muddiness of the ordinary body has disappeared, and the hues are all brilliant and clearly marked, good and bad alike. It is an intensification of the life in various directions.

It will be noticed that the blue of devotion is also distinctly improved, and even (so much has the nature been temporarily elevated) a touch of pale violet appears at the summit of the ovoid, indicating a capacity of response to a really high and unselfish ideal. The yellow of intellect, however, has entirely vanished for the time—which I suppose would be considered by the cynical as characteristic of the condition!

It seems scarcely possible that after all this brilliant development the man should sink back again into the condition indicated in Plate X., yet in the majority of cases this is what occurs, though naturally the amount of crimson has considerably augmented, and it is clearer in hue than before. This experience of being "in love" is assuredly a valuable one for the ego, and gives him a definite forward impulse, even though there may often be associated with it much that is undesirable. The intensely strong and unselfish affection often felt by children for those somewhat older than themselves is a very powerful factor in their progress, since it is usually an unmixed benefit, free from all associations connected with the lower animal nature. Even though such affection may seem transitory, and may change its object more than once as years roll on, it is nevertheless very real while it lasts, and it serves a noble purpose in preparing the vehicle to respond more readily to the stronger vibrations which are yet in the future—just as the unset blossom of the fruit-tree, which seems to come to nothing, in reality has its function, since it not only looks exceedingly beautiful at the time, but also helps to draw up the sap for the fruit that is to come.

The Irritable Man

We turn now to the consideration of the

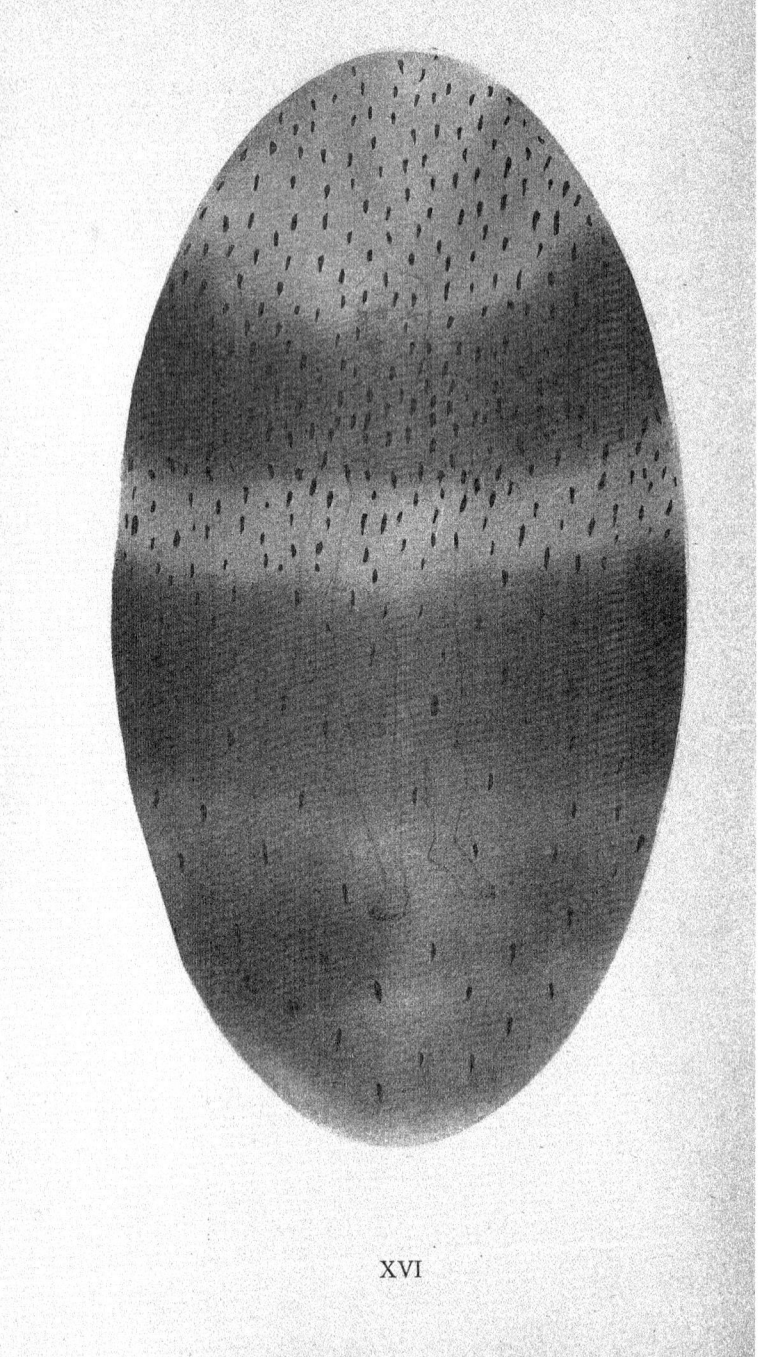

XVI

manner in which certain special types of character exhibit themselves in the bodies of the man. The case of the irritable man is a good specimen of this. His astral body will usually show a broad band of scarlet in one of its prominent features, as we see in Plate XVI. But what especially differentiates him from other men is the presence in all parts of the astral body of little floating flecks of scarlet, somewhat like notes of exclamation. These are the result of little accessions of irritation at the small worries which are constantly occurring in ordinary life. Every time any little trifle goes wrong—when his coffee is cold, when he loses his tram, or when the baby upsets its milk bottle—the irritable man gives vent to an impatient or angry exclamation, and a tiny scarlet flash shows his uncontrolled feeling. In some cases these little messengers of undisciplined temper fly outwards towards the person who is supposed to be responsible for whatever has gone wrong; but in many others they simply remain floating within him, suspended in the matter of the astral body, and presenting the appearance shown in our illustration. These spots gradually fade away, but their places are taken by others for the irritable man is never at a loss for subjects of annoyance.

manner in which certain special types of character exhibit themselves in the bodies of the man. The case of the irritable man is a good specimen of these. His astral body will usually show a broad band of scarlet as one of its prominent features, as we see in Plate XVI. But what especially differentiates him from other men is the presence in all parts of the astral body of little floating flecks of scarlet, somewhat like notes of exclamation. These are the result of little accessions of irritation at the small worries which are constantly occurring in ordinary life. Every time any little trifle goes wrong—when his coffee is cold, when he misses his train, or when the baby upsets the ink bottle—the irritable man gives vent to an impatient or angry exclamation, and a tiny scarlet flash shows the uncontrolled feeling. In some cases these little messengers of undisciplined temper fly outwards towards the person who is supposed to be responsible for whatever has gone wrong; but in many others they simply remain floating within him, suspended in the matter of the astral body, and presenting the appearance shown in our illustration. These spots gradually fade away, but their places are taken by others, for the irritable man is never at a loss for subjects of annoyance.

The Miser

Another striking, but happily less common, spectacle, is that which is imaged for us in Plate XVII. The background differs somewhat from the ordinary astral body, for there is a total absence of devotion, and far less than the normal proportion of affection. Avarice, selfishness, deceit and adaptability (or perhaps, rather, cunning) are all intensified, but, on the other hand, there is very little sensuality. The most remarkable characteristic, however, is to be seen in the curious series of parallel horizontal lines which bar the oval, and give the impression that the man within is confined in a cage. These bars are of a deep brown colour, almost burnt sienna, level and clearly marked as to their upper edge, but shading off into a sort of cloud below. This is an illustration of a confirmed miser, and naturally so extreme a case is not very common; but a large number of people seem to have some of the elements of the miser in their nature, and show them by an intensification of the colour of avarice and by one or two such bars in the upper part of the astral body, though few are so completely confined as is this specimen. This vice of avarice seems to have the effect of completely arresting development for the time, and it is very difficult

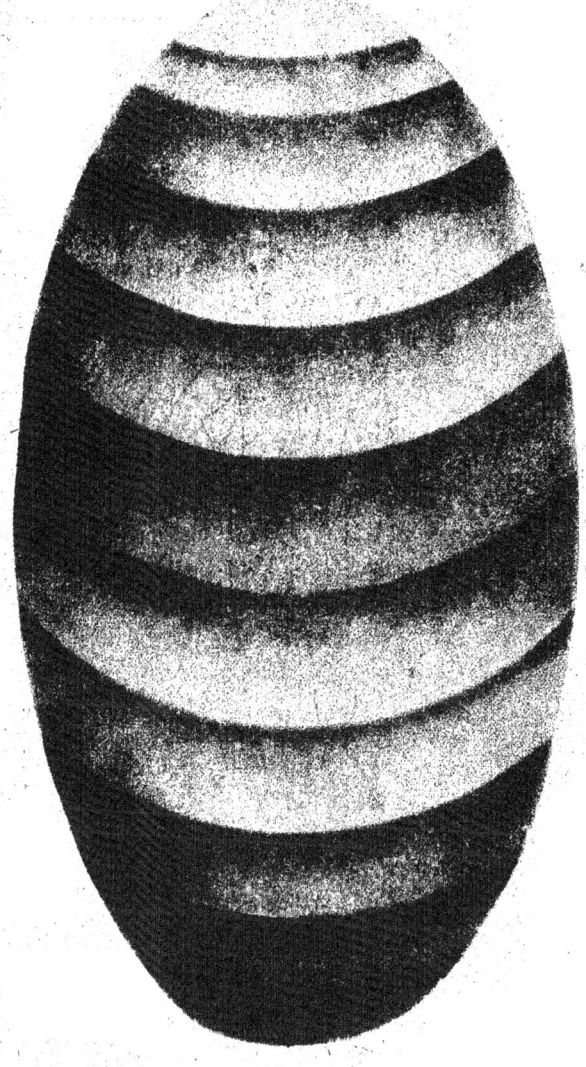

XVII

The Miser

Another striking, but happily less common, spectacle, is that which is imaged for us in Plate XVII. The background differs somewhat from the ordinary astral body, for there is a total absence of devotion, and far less than the normal proportion of affection. Avarice, selfishness, deceit and adaptability (or perhaps, rather, cunning) are all intensified, but, on the other hand, there is very little sensuality. The most remarkable characteristic, however, is to be seen in the curious series of parallel horizontal lines which bar the oval, and give the impression that the man within is confined in a cage. These bars are of a deep brown colour, almost burnt sienna, level and clearly marked as to their upper edge, but shading off into a sort of cloud below. This is an illustration of a confirmed miser, and naturally so extreme a case is not very common; but a large number of people seem to have some of the elements of the miser in their nature, and show them by an intensification of the colour of avarice and by one or two such bars in the upper part of the astral body, though few are so completely confined as is this specimen. This vice of avarice seems to have the effect of completely arresting development for the time, and it is very difficult

XVII

to shake off when once it has gained a firm hold upon the personality.

Deep Depression

The astral body shown in Plate XVIII. is in many ways similar to the last. Here, however, we have dull grey lines instead of the brown, and the whole effect is indescribably gloomy and depressing to the observer. It does not seem that in this case any qualities are necessarily absent; we have simply the ordinary colours of the body as a background, but all are veiled by these heavy weeping lines. Our picture represents a person during a period of extreme depression, and naturally there are very many intermediate stages between this and the healthy astral body. A man may have only a few bars of depression, and even they may be but transient; or in slighter and less persistent cases, the heavy cloud may hardly have time to arrange itself in lines at all. Yet there are only too many who yield themselves to these feelings, and allow the fog of despair to close round them until all the world looks black; not realising that in doing so they are not only seriously delaying their own evolution and losing manifold opportunities, but are also causing unnecessary suffering and injury to all those near to them. No psychic condition is more infectious than this feeling of depression; its vibrations radiate in all directions and introduce their slackening, deadening effects into every astral body within reach, whether the ego to which that astral body belongs is in incarnation or not. The man who gives way to despondency is thus a nuisance and a danger alike to the living and the dead, for in these days of overstrain and nervous worry most people find it very difficult to resist the contagion of these funereal vibrations. (The only man who is proof against such dire influences is he who understands something of the purpose of life, who regards it from the philosophical and common-sense standpoint, and realises that it is his duty to be happy, since the Logos intends that he should be so. The student of Theosophy should be instantly distinguishable from the rest of the world by his absolute serenity under all possible difficulties, and his radiant joy in helping others.) Fortunately good influences can be spread abroad just as readily as evil ones, (and the man who is wise enough to be happy will become a centre of happiness for others, a veritable sun, shedding light and joy on all around him, and to this extent acting as a fellow-worker together with God, who is the source of all joy.) In this way we may all of us help to break up these gloomy bars of depression, and set the soul within them free in the glorious sunlight of the divine love.

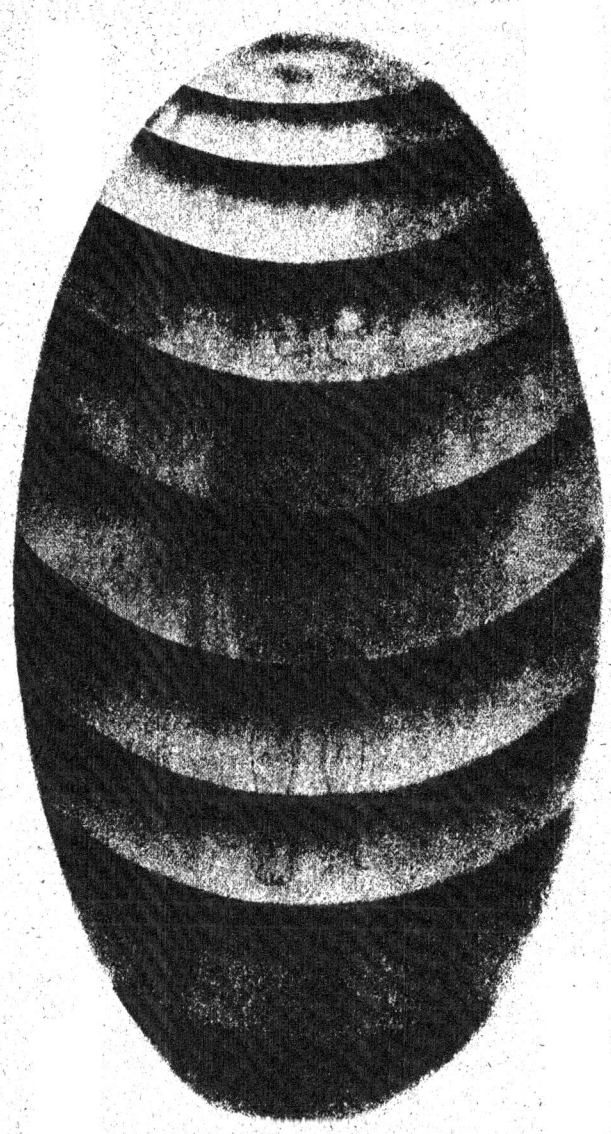

xviii

and introduce their slackening, deadening effects into every astral body within reach, whether the ego to which that astral body belongs is in incarnation or not. The man who gives way to despondency is thus a nuisance and a danger alike to the living and the dead, for in these days of overstrain and nervous worry most people find it very difficult to resist the contagion of these funereal vibrations. (The only man who is proof against such dire influences is he who understands something of the purpose of life, who regards it from the philosophical and common-sense standpoint, and realises that it is his duty to be happy, since the Logos intends that he should be so. The student of Theosophy should be instantly distinguishable from the rest of the world by his absolute serenity under all possible difficulties, and his radiant joy in helping others.) Fortunately good influences can be spread abroad just as readily as evil ones, (and the man who is wise enough to be happy will become a centre of happiness for others, a veritable sun, shedding light and joy on all around him, and to this extent acting as a fellow-worker together God, who is the source of all joy.) In this we may all of us help to break up these gloomy bars of depression, and set the soul within them free in the glorious sunlight of the divine love.

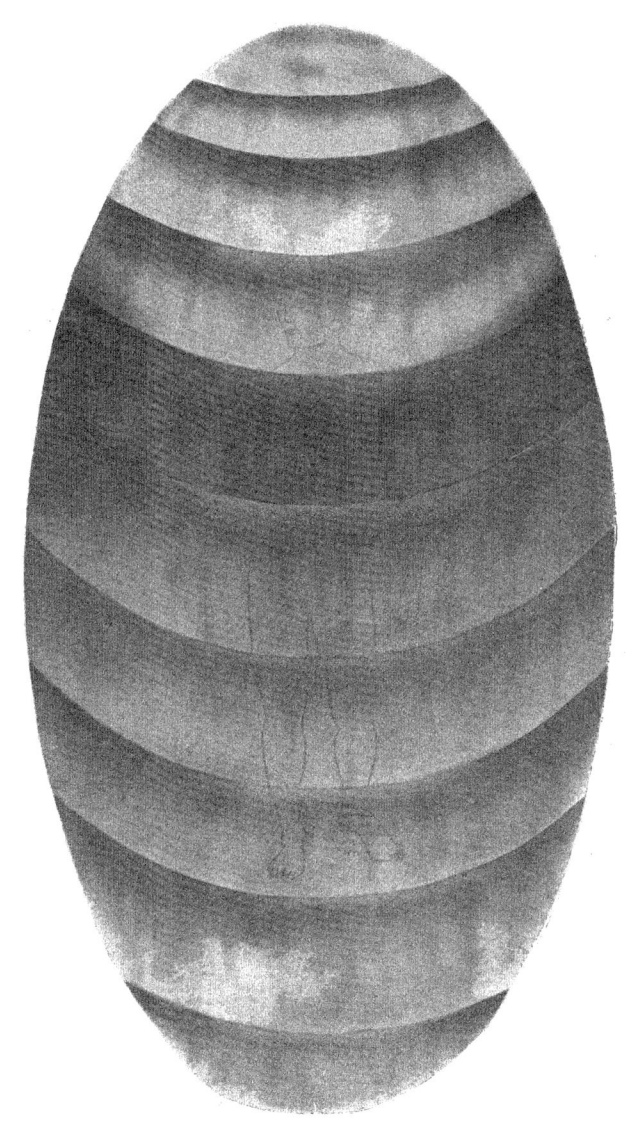

XVIII

The Devotional Type

It will be useful for us to close our list of special cases among astral bodies by examining two very distinct types, from the comparison of which a good deal may be learnt. The first of these is illustrated in Plate XIX., and we may call him the devotional man. His characteristics present themselves through the medium of his colours, and we see that he possesses the faint touch of violet which suggests the possibility of his response to the presentment of a high ideal. His most prominent feature is the unusual development of the blue, showing strong religious feeling; but unfortunately only a very small proportion of this is the pure light blue of unselfish devotion, the majority being of a dark and somewhat muddy hue, suggesting the admixture of a good deal of desire for personal gain.

The very small proportion of yellow tells us that he has very little intelligence to direct his devotion into reasonable channels, or to save him from degenerating into senseless bigotry. He has a fair proportion of affection and adaptability, though not of very high order; but the amount of sensuality expressed is much above the average, and deceit and selfishness are also very prominent. It is a remarkable fact that extreme sensuality and the devotional temperament are so frequently seen in association; it would suggest that there must be some hidden connection between them—or it may be simply that both are characteristic of a man who lives chiefly in his feelings, and is governed by them instead of trying to control them by reason. Another point to which attention should be paid is the irregularity in the distribution of the colours and the vagueness of their outline; they all melt into one another, and there are no clear lines of demarcation anywhere. This also is very characteristic of the vagueness of the devotional man's conceptions.

It will be understood that in this case, as in all the others of this chapter, we are dealing merely with variants of the ordinary person. Consequently this is the astral body of an ordinary and non-intellectual religious man—not in the least that of the developed religious man whose devotion is evoked by full comprehension and guided by reason.

The Scientific Type

The observer can hardly fail to be struck by the contrast between the body illustrated in Plate XX. and that which we have just described. In Plate XIX. we see the principal features are devotion (of a sort) and sensuality, and a very small modicum of intellect is shown; in Plate XX. we have no devotion at all, and far

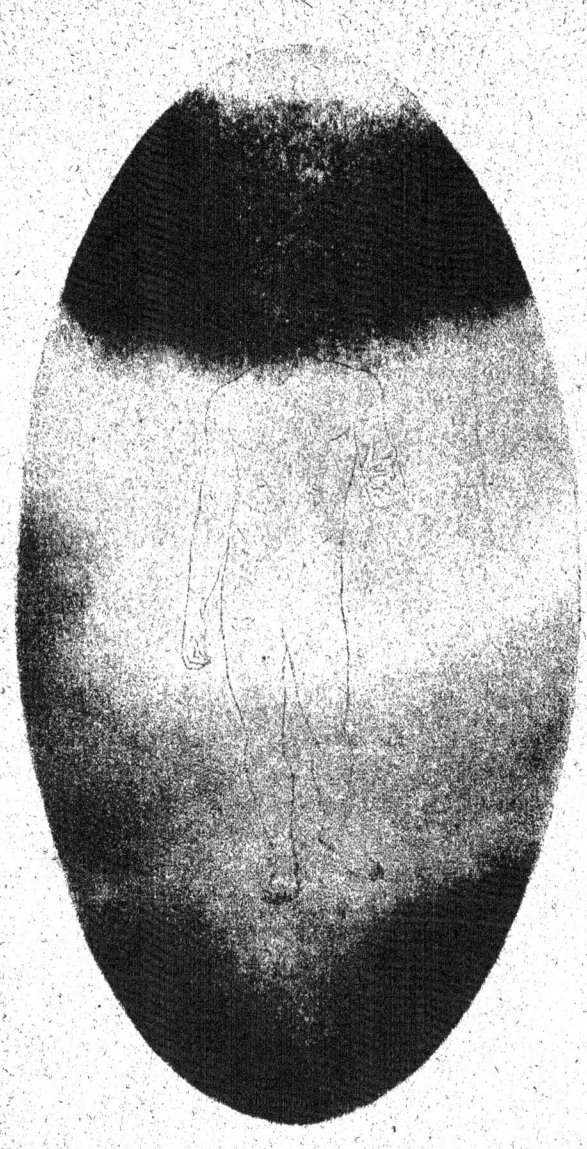

XIX

so frequently seen in association; it would suggest that there must be some hidden connection between them—or it may be simply that both are characteristic of a man who lives chiefly in his feelings, and is governed by them instead of trying to control them by reason. Another point to which attention should be paid is the irregularity in the distribution of the colours and the vagueness of their outline; they all melt into one another, and there are no clear lines of demarcation anywhere. This also is very characteristic of the vagueness of the devotional man's conceptions.

It will be understood that in this case, as in all the others of this chapter, we are dealing merely with variants of the ordinary person. Consequently this is the astral body of an ordinary and non-intellectual religious man—not in the least that of the developed religious man whose devotion is evoked by full comprehension and guided by reason.

The Scientific Type

The observer can hardly fail to be struck by the contrast between the body illustrated in Plate XX. and that which we have just described. In Plate XIX. we see the principal features are devotion (of a sort) and sensuality, and a very small modicum of intellect is shown; in Plate XX. we have no devotion at all, and far

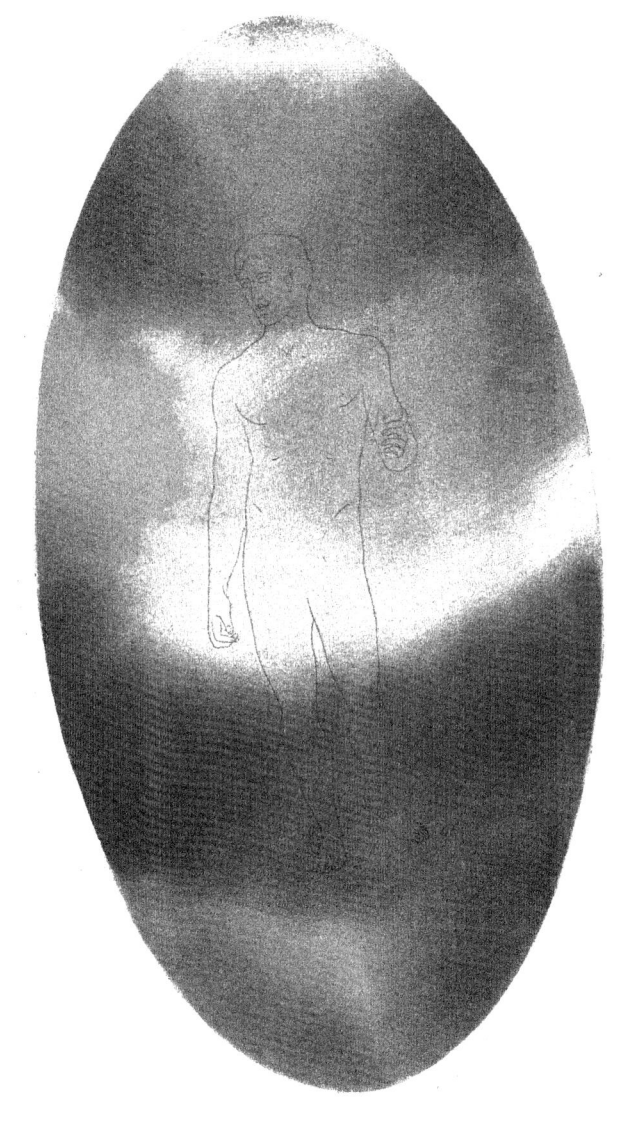

XIX

less than the average amount of sensuality, but the intellect is developed to a very abnormal degree. Affection and adaptability are both somewhat small in quantity and poor in quality, being apparently overshadowed by the intellectual development, as the man is not yet sufficiently advanced to possess all these qualities equally in their higher forms. There is a good deal of selfishness and avarice, and a certain capability of jealousy is also apparent. But the great feature of this man is the large proportion of golden yellow, showing a well-developed intelligence directed principally to the attainment of knowledge. A huge cone of bright orange rising in the midst of it indicates the presence of much pride and ambition in connection with that knowledge, but still the shade of the yellow precludes the idea that the intellect is debased to merely selfish ends.

It should be noticed also that the scientific and orderly habit of mind has a distinct influence upon the arrangement of the astral colours; they tend to fall into regular bands, and the lines of demarcation between them are decidedly more definite than in the previous illustration.

It is evident that the bodies pictured in Plates XIX. and XX. give us examples of two varieties of unequal development; and while each has its good points, each also has decided disadvantages. We shall now proceed to the consideration of the vehicles of the more developed man who possesses all these various qualities to a much greater extent, but has them well balanced, so that each supports and strengthens the other, instead of dominating or stifling it.

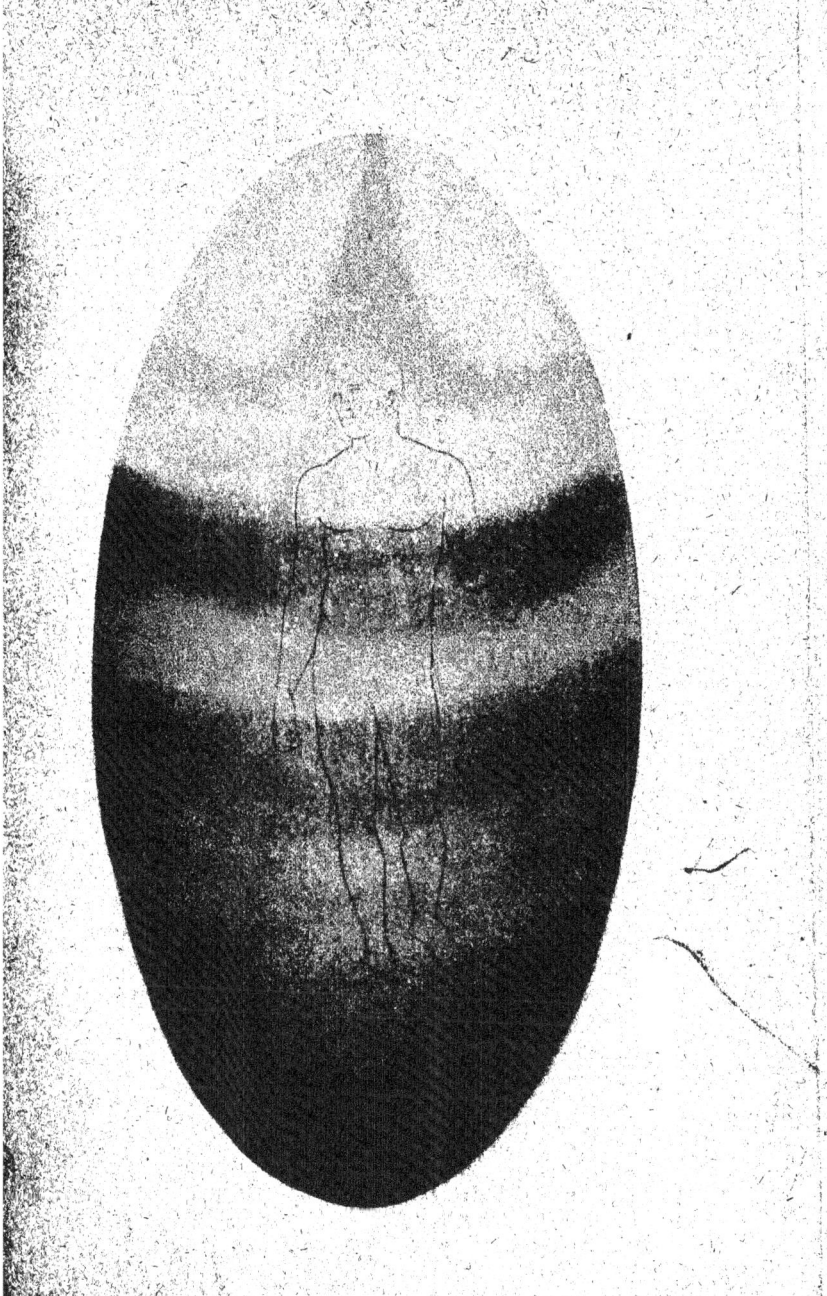

XX

good points, each also has decided disadvantages. We shall now proceed to the consideration of the vehicles of the more developed man who possesses all these various qualities to a much greater extent, but has them well balanced, so that each supports and strengthens the other, instead of dominating or killing it.

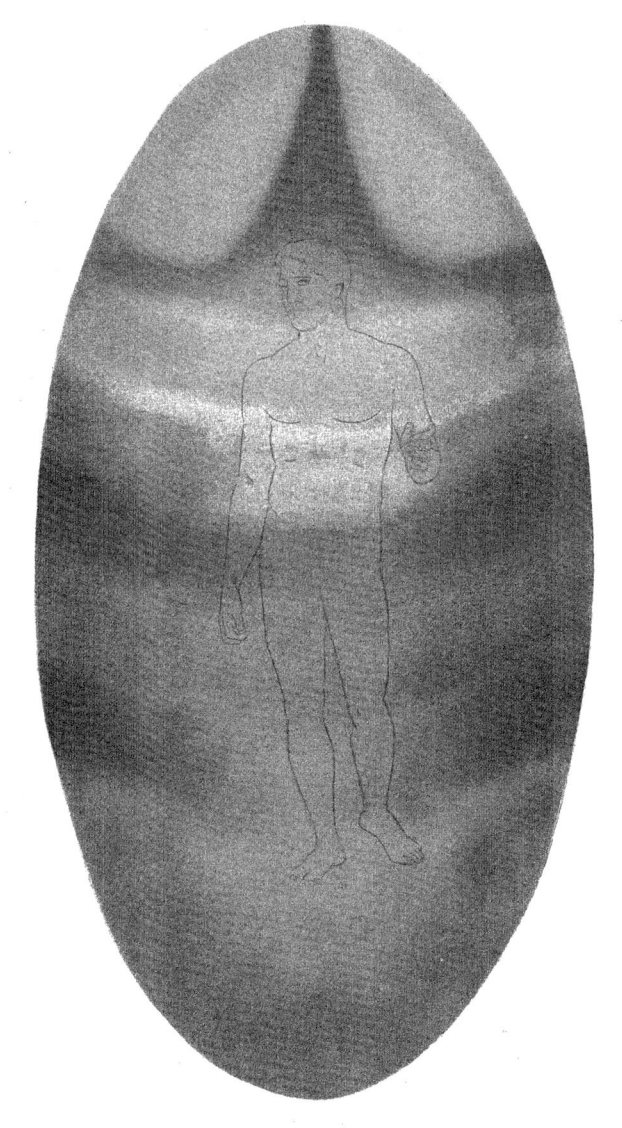

XX

Chapter XVIII

THE DEVELOPED MAN

THE term "developed" is a relative one, so it will be well to explain exactly what is here meant by it. The vehicles illustrated under this heading are such as might be possessed by any pure-minded person who had definitely and intelligently "set his affection on things above, and not on things of earth." They are not those of one already far advanced upon the path which leads to adeptship, for in that case we should find a considerable difference in size as well as in arrangement. But they do distinctly imply that the man of whom they are expressions is a seeker after the higher truth, one who has risen above mere earthly aims, and is living for an ideal. Among such some may be found who are especially advanced in one direction, and some in another; this is an evenly-balanced man—simply a fair average of those who are at the level which I describe.

We may first examine Plate XXI., which

represents for us his causal body. By comparing this with Plates V. and VIII. we shall see what the man's progress has been, and how it is expressed in his appearance. We observe that by this time many beautiful qualities have been developed within him, for the glorious iridescent film is now filled with the most lovely colours, typifying for us the higher forms of love, devotion and sympathy, aided by an intellect refined and spiritualised, and by aspirations reaching ever towards the divine. Let me quote from the sixth of our Theosophical manuals, p. 80 :—

"Composed of matter inconceivably fine, delicate and ethereal, intensely alive and pulsating with living fire, it becomes as its evolution proceeds a radiant globe of flashing colours, its high vibrations sending ripples of changing hues over its surface—hues of which earth knows nothing — brilliant, soft and luminous beyond the power of language to describe. Take the colours of an Egyptian sunset and add to them the wonderful softness of an English sky at eventide—raise these as high above themselves in light and translucency and splendour as they are above the colours given by the cakes of a child's paint-box—and even then none who have not seen can image the beauty of these radiant

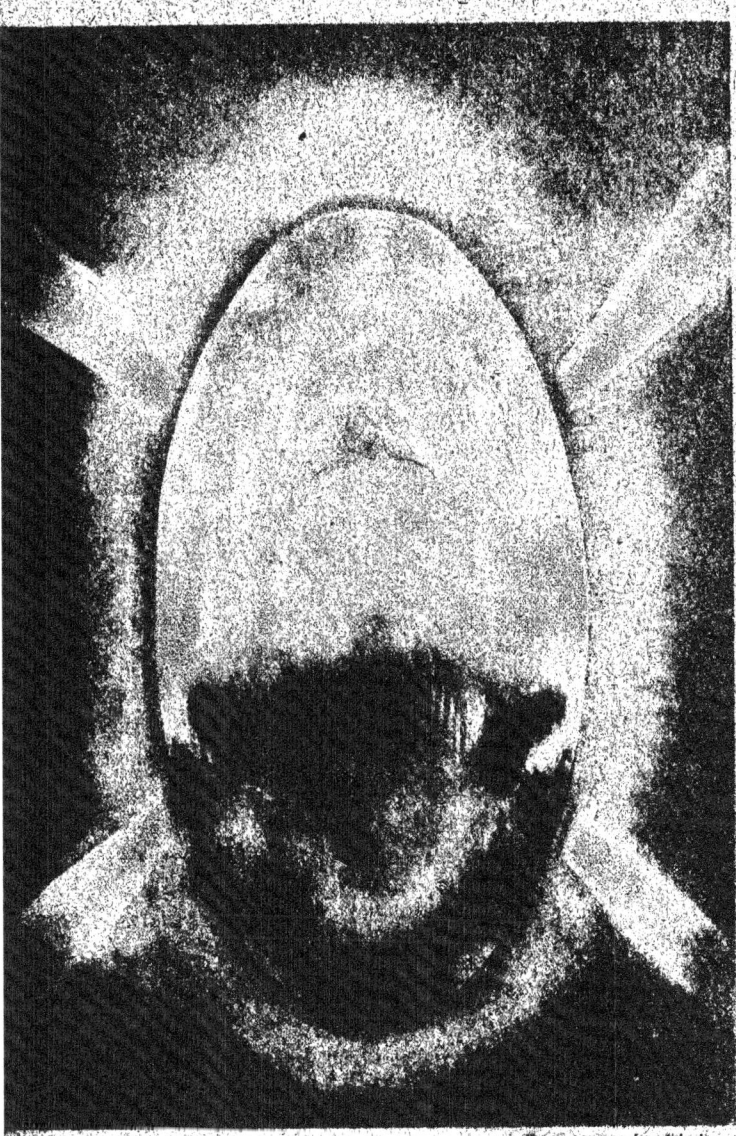

XXI

represents for us his causal body. By comparing this with Plates V. and VIII. we shall see what the man's progress has been, and how it is expressed in his appearance. We observe that by this time many beautiful qualities have been developed within him, for the glorious iridescent film is now filled with the most lovely colours, typifying for us the higher forms of love, devotion and sympathy, aided by an intellect refined and spiritualised, and by aspirations tending ever towards the divine. Let me quote from the sixth of our Theosophical Manuals on The Devachanic Plane:—

"Composed of matter incomparably more delicate and ethereal, instinct, alive and pulsating with living fire, it becomes as its evolution proceeds a radiant globe of flashing colours, its high vibrations sending ripples of changing hues over its surface—hues of which earth knows nothing — brilliant, soft and luminous beyond the power of language to describe. Take the colours of an Egyptian sunset and add to them the wonderful softness of an English sky at eventide—raise these as high above themselves in light and translucency and splendour as they are above the colours given by the cakes of a child's paint-box—and even then none who have not seen can image the beauty of these radiant

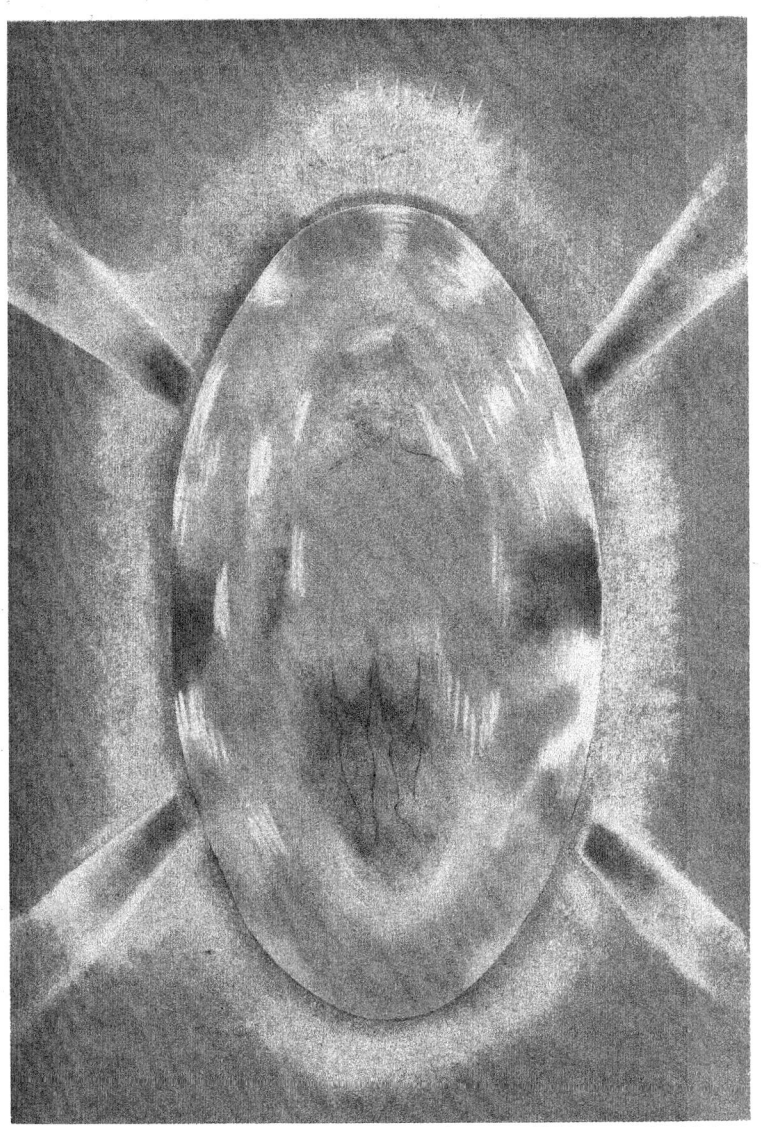

Photochromogravure, Lyons & London

orbs which flash into the field of clairvoyant vision as it is lifted to the level of this supernal world.

"All these causal bodies are filled with living fire drawn from a higher plane, with which the globe appears to be connected by a quivering thread of intense light, vividly recalling to the mind the words of the stanzas of Dzyan, 'The spark hangs from the flame by the finest thread of Fohat'; and as the soul grows and is able to receive more and more from the inexhaustible ocean of the Divine Spirit which pours down through the thread as a channel, the latter expands and gives wider passage to the flood, till on the next sub-plane it might be imaged as a water-spout connecting earth and sky, and higher still as itself a great globe through which rushes the living spring, until the causal body seems to melt into the inpouring light. Once more the stanza says it for us: 'The thread between the watcher and his shadow becomes more strong and radiant with every change. The morning sunlight has changed into noon-day glory. This is thy present wheel, said the flame to the spark. Thou art myself, my image and my shadow. I have clothed myself in thee, and thou art my vâhan to the day, "Be-with-us," when thou shalt re-become myself and others, thyself and me.'"

How hopeless it seems to try to represent all this glory on paper! Yet our artist has skilfully contrived to suggest that which no brush could paint and however far even the cleverest physical image may be from that transcendent reality, it at least gives our imagination a starting-point from which we may try to build up a conception.

We must not omit to notice one of the grandest characteristics of the developed man—his capacity to serve as a channel for higher force. It will be seen that from his causal body streams of this force pour out in various directions, for his attitude of unselfishness, of helpfulness and readiness to give, makes it possible for the divine strength to descend upon him in steady stream, and through him to reach many who are not yet strong enough to receive it directly. Thus to become one of God's almoners is indeed a privilege worth working for, yet it is within our reach if we will but try for it.

The crown of brilliant sparks which ascends from the upper part of the body indicates the activity of spiritual aspiration, and adds very greatly to the beauty and dignity of the man's appearance. This rises constantly from the causal body, no matter how the lower man may be occupied on the physical plane: for when the

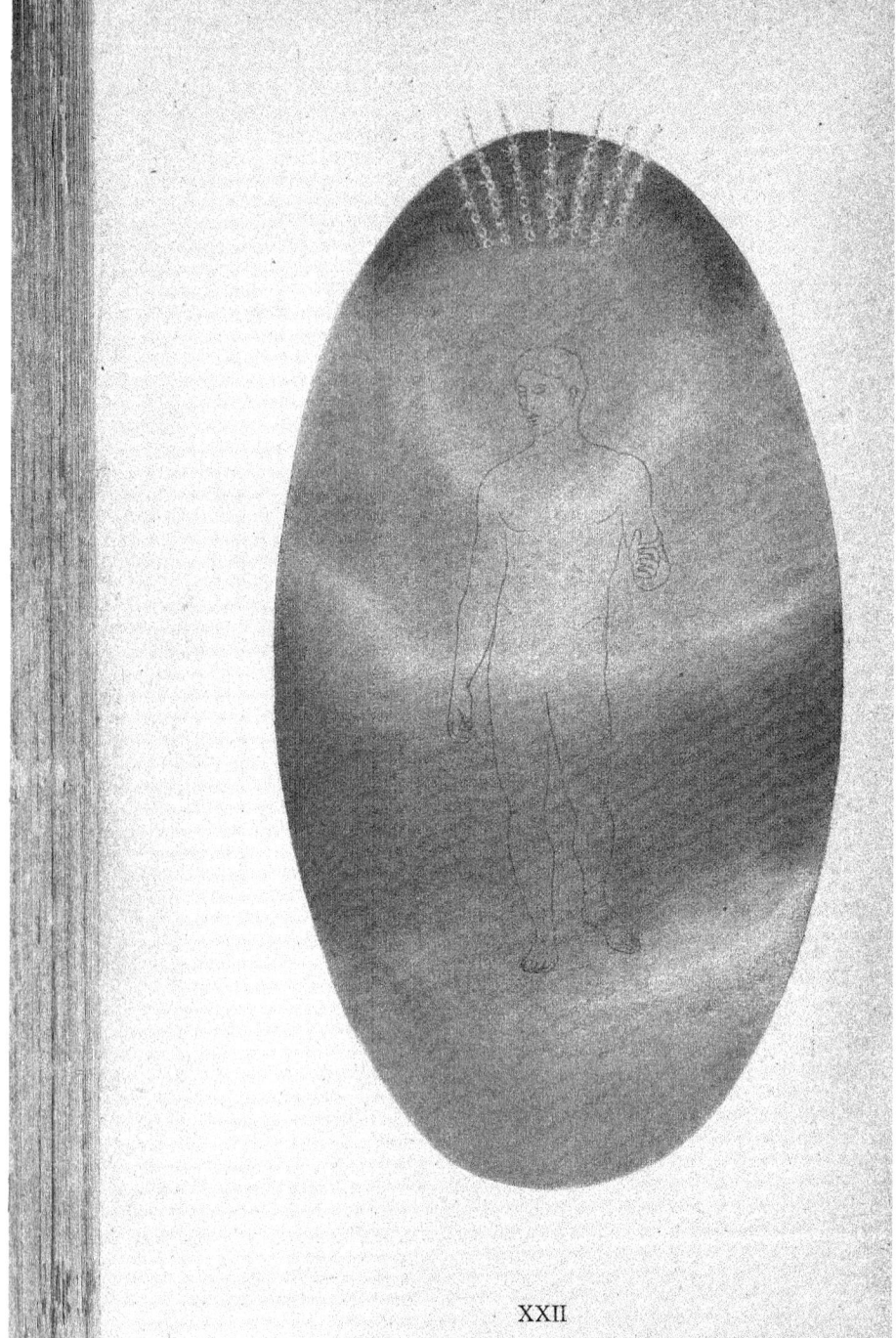

XXII

he may at the same time be inspiring on lower planes. We must never forget how small and partial an expression of the self even the noblest personality can be; so that as soon as the higher man begins to look round him, he finds almost unlimited possibilities opening before him, of which in this cramped physical life we can form no idea.

This very upward rushing of spiritual aspiration, which makes so glorious a crown for our developed man, is itself the channel through which the divine power descends; so that the fuller and stronger his aspirations become, the larger is the measure of the grace from on high.

His Mental Body

It can hardly fail to strike the observer as we come to deal with the more developed man, that his various vehicles are not only all of them greatly refined and improved, but they are also very much more like one another. Allowing for the difference between what we may call the octaves of the colour—between the hues belonging

soul of man is once awakened upon his own level, and is beginning to understand something of himself and his relation to the divine, he looks ever upwards towards the source from which he came, totally irrespective of any activities which he may at the same time be inspiring on lower planes. We must never forget how small and partial an expression of the self even the noblest personality can be; so that as soon as the higher man begins to look round him, he finds almost unlimited possibilities opening before him, of which in this cramped physical life we can form no idea.

This very upward rushing of spiritual aspiration, which makes so glorious a crown for our developed man, is itself the channel through which the divine power descends; so that the fuller and stronger his aspirations become, the larger is the measure of the grace from on high.

His Mental Body

It can hardly fail to strike the observer as we come to deal with the more developed man, that his various vehicles are not only all of them greatly refined and improved, but they are also very much more like one another. Allowing for the difference between what we may call the octaves of the colour—between the hues belonging to the lower and the higher levels of the mental plane—Plate XXII. is almost a reproduction of Plate XXI.; and the resemblance between Plates XXII. and XXIII. is perhaps even more marked, though in comparing them we have to remember that astral colours are again of a different octave from even the lower mental.

Another useful comparison to make is that between Plates XXII., IX. and VI., in order that we may see how the evolution from the savage to the unselfish man shows itself in the mind-body. It will appear upon examination that pride, anger and selfishness have altogether disappeared, and that the remaining colours have not only so expanded as to fill the whole oval, but have also so improved in tone as to give quite a different impression. Every one of them is more refined and delicate, for all thought of self has vanished from them; and in addition has appeared the pure violet with the golden stars, which indicates the acquisition of new and greater qualities. The power from above, which we saw radiating out through his causal body, acts also through the mental vehicle, though with somewhat less force. This is on the whole a very fine mental body, already well developed, and having within it every promise of rapid progress along the Path, when the time for that shall come.

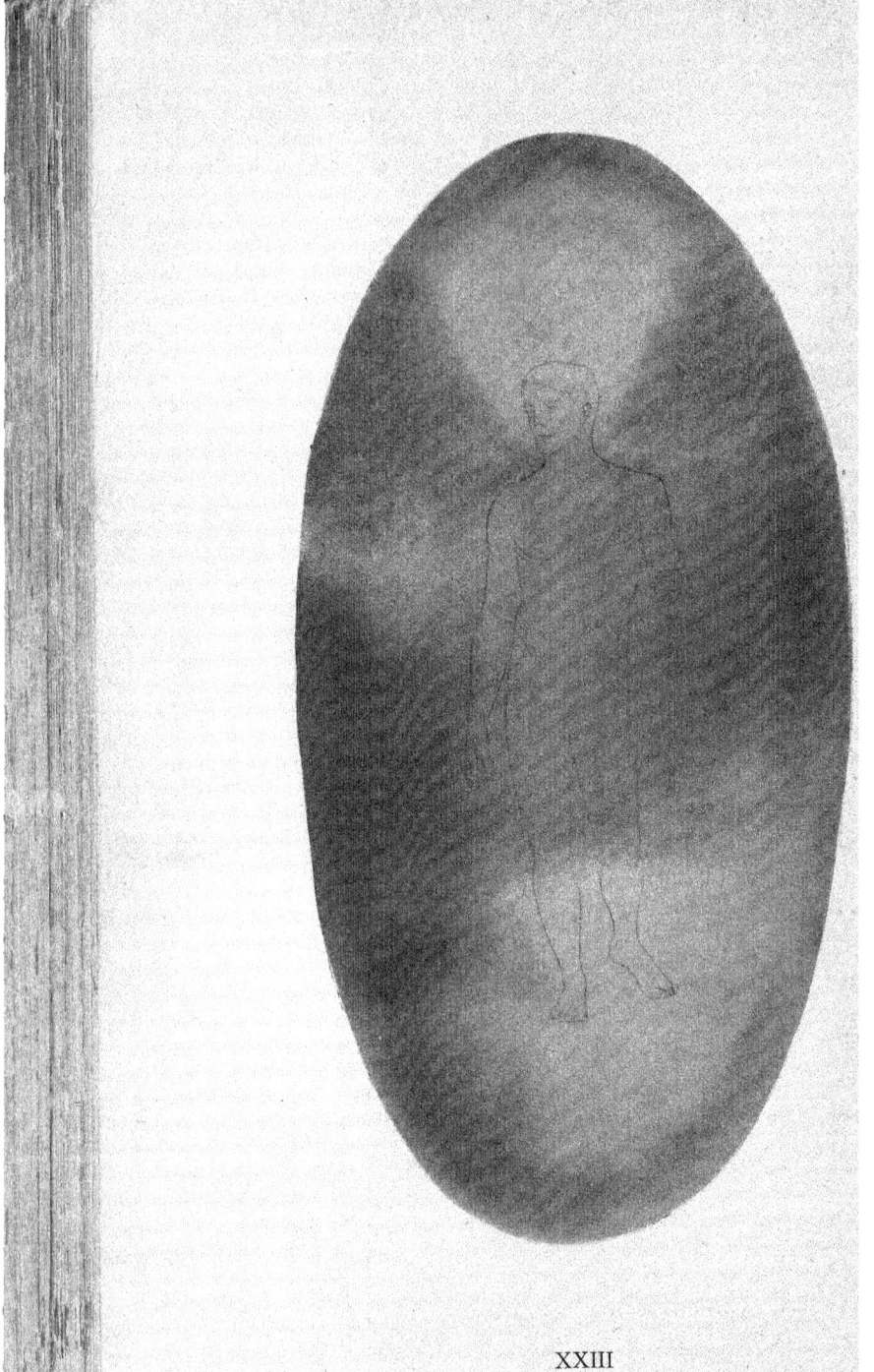

XXIII

away from the firm base of reason by wild surges of emotion. Since he is not yet definitely on the Path, he will no doubt still be subject to occasional irritability, and to undesirable cravings of various sorts. But he knows enough now to repress these lower manifestations, to maintain a struggle against them whenever they appear, instead of yielding to them. So though they may temporarily change his astral body, they will hardly make any permanent impression upon it as against the much stronger vibrations of his higher qualities.

In exactly the same way, at a still later stage of progress, the mental body itself becomes a reflection of the causal, since the man learns to follow solely the promptings of the higher self, and to guide his reason exclusively by them.

This illustration brings clearly before us an interesting fact connected with the yellow light, which signifies intellect. When this colour is

His Astral Body

His astral body, which is pictured in Plate XXIII., will at once be seen to resemble the mental vehicle very closely. It is, in fact, little more than a reflection of it in the grosser matter of the astral plane. This indicates that the man has his desires thoroughly under the control of the mind, and is no longer liable to be swept away from the firm base of reason by wild surges of emotion. Since he is not yet definitely on the Path, he will no doubt still be subject to occasional irritability, and to undesirable cravings of various sorts. But he knows enough now to repress these lower manifestations, to maintain a struggle against them whenever they appear, instead of yielding to them. So though they may temporarily change his astral body, they will hardly make any permanent impression upon it as against the much stronger vibrations of his higher qualities.

In exactly the same way, at a still later stage of progress, the mental body itself becomes a reflection of the causal, since the man learns to follow solely the promptings of the higher self, and to guide his reason exclusively by them.

This illustration brings clearly before us an interesting fact connected with the yellow light, which signifies intellect. When this colour is present in the oval, it invariably shows itself in the upper part of it, in the neighbourhood of the head; consequently it is the origin of the idea of the nimbus or glory round the head of a saint, since this yellow is much the most conspicuous of the colours of the astral body, and the one most easily perceived by anyone who is approaching the verge of clairvoyance. Also, even without astral sight it may occasionally be perceived; for when any person of some development is making a special effort of any kind, as, for example, in preaching or lecturing, the intellectual faculties are in unusual activity, and the yellow glow is therefore intensified. In some cases which I have seen, it has passed the bounds of physical visibility, and been seen by many who had no power of higher sight than that of this plane. In such a case, it is not that the astral vibration slackens until it sinks below the line which separates it from the physical, but that it becomes so much more vigorous than usual that it is able to arouse a sympathetic vibration even in the coarse and heavy matter of the physical plane. No doubt it was either from occasional glimpses of this phenomenon or from traditions derived from those who could see, that our mediæval painters derived the idea of the glory round the head of the saint. It may be remembered that in the nimbus of the Christ a cross is usually drawn; and this also is strictly within the probabilities, from the point of view of occult investigation, for it has often been observed that in the auras of very highly-developed persons various geometrical figures present themselves, signifying certain elevated and far-reaching thoughts. See Mrs. Besant's article on "Thought-Forms" in *Lucifer* for September 1896.

The student will find it useful to compare these illustrations carefully one with another; first, to examine each causal body in connection with the mental and astral bodies which are partial expressions of it, in order to understand the connection between these different vehicles; and secondly, to compare the three astral bodies in Plates VII., X., and XXIII., in order to understand how progress shows itself in the desire-body, which is naturally much the easiest of the various vehicles to see clairvoyantly, and in fact the only one which the ordinary psychically-developed person is at all likely to see. The same comparison should be instituted between Plates VI., IX., and XXII., and also between Plates V., VIII., and XXI. to study the progress of the man as manifested in his higher bodies.

Among our Theosophical literature we have many books which treat of the other side of all this evolution, and catalogue the moral qualifications required at its various stages. This is a subject of the very deepest interest, though somewhat outside of the scope of this little work. Those who wish to study it should turn to *Invisible Helpers*, Chapters XIV. to XVI., and then read Mrs. Besant's books *In the Outer Court* and *The Path of Discipleship*.

From those books some idea may be gained not only of the conditions of progress, but of its goal and of the glorious future that awaits us when we shall have fulfilled those conditions — when after many incarnations upon this grand old world of ours we shall at last have learnt the lessons which its physical life is meant to teach us. Then we shall have attained that "resurrection of the dead" after which St. Paul was so earnestly striving, for we shall be free alike from death and from birth, we shall have transcended the cycle of necessity, and shall be free for evermore—free to help our fellow-men along the path that we have trodden, until they also gain the light and the victory which is ours. For this attainment is for every man, and to reach it is only a question of time, however young a soul may be. There is for man no doubt about "salvation," since there is nothing except his own error and ignorance from which any man needs to be saved; there is for him not even an "eternal hope," but an eternal certainty. All

shall attain, because that is God's will for them,
that is the sole object for which He called them
into existence at all. Even already the world is
progressing, and the powers are beginning to
develope; and assuredly this morning sunrise
shall increase into noonday glory. To the vistas
of advancement that stretch before man, our
keenest sight can see no end; we know only
that they extend into splendours indescribable
illimitable, and divine.

CHAPTER XIX

THE HEALTH-AURA

HITHERTO we have been dealing exclusively with those bodies of man which are connected with the higher planes, but our subject would not be completely treated if we omitted all reference to the minutely subdivided physical matter which is seen by clairvoyant sight to be part of the aura of man. Much of that matter is in the etheric state, and constitutes what is often called the etheric double. This is not in any sense a separate vehicle, but must be considered simply as part of the physical body. It is clearly visible to the clairvoyant as a mass of faintly luminous violet-grey mist, interpenetrating the denser part of the physical body, and extending very slightly beyond it, as will be seen in Plates XXIV. and XXV. This etheric matter is the link between the astral and the physical, but it has also a very important function as the vehicle of the vital force on the physical plane.

This vital force is poured upon us from the

reference to the minutely subdivided physical matter which is seen by clairvoyant sight to be part of the aura of man. Much of that matter is in the etheric state, and constitutes what is often called the etheric double. This is not in any sense a separate vehicle, but must be considered simply as part of the physical body. It is clearly visible to the clairvoyant as a mass of faintly luminous violet-grey mist, interpenetrating the denser part of the physical body, and extending very slightly beyond it, as will be seen in Plates XXIV. and XXV. This etheric matter is the link between the astral and the physical, but it has also a very important function as the vehicle of the vital force on the physical plane.

This vital force is poured upon us from

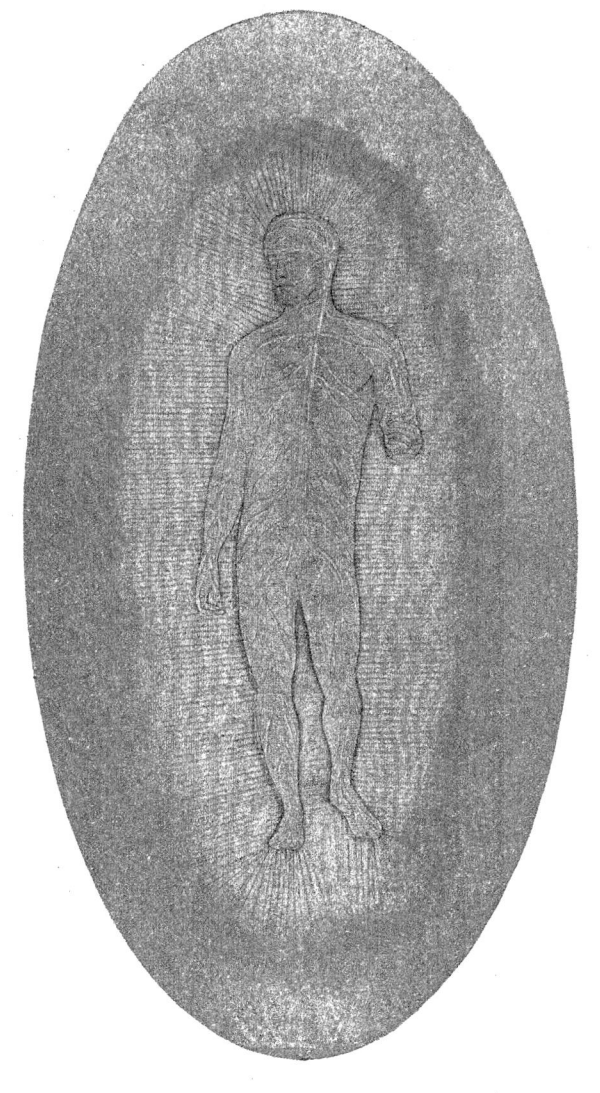

XXIV

sun, which is the source of life in this inner sense as well as by means of its light and heat in the outer world. The earth's atmosphere is full of this force at all times, though it is in special activity in brilliant sunlight; and it is only by absorbing it that our physical bodies are able to live. The absorption of this vital energy is one of the functions of the etheric art of that organ which we call the spleen; and that organ possesses the curious property of specializing and transmuting the force as it passes through it, so that it presents a totally different appearance.

The force itself is naturally invisible, like all other forces; but as it exists around us in the atmosphere it clothes itself in millions of tiny particles which are colourless though intensely active. After it has been absorbed into the human body through the spleen, however, these particles take on a beautiful pale rose-colour, and they flow in a constant stream over and through the whole body along the nerves, in the same manner as the blood-corpuscles flow along the arteries and veins, the brain being the centre of this nervous circulation. An attempt is made in our illustrations to represent the general appearance of this stream, but this must not of course be supposed to be an accurate map of the nervous system.

It is evident that this flow is necessary to the

proper working of the nerves, for when it is withdrawn there is no sensation. We know how a limb may be so numbed by cold as to be absolutely insensible to the touch; and the reason of such insensibility is that the vital force is no longer flowing through it. It might be supposed that it was rather due to the failure of the circulation of the blood, but those who have studied mesmerism are aware that one of the commonest experiments is to produce similar insensibility in a limb by magnetic passes. This does not at all interfere with the circulation of the blood, for the limb remains warm; but it does check the circulation of the subject's life-fluid, and substitutes for it that of the magnetizer. The nerves of the subject are still there, and (so far as physical sight can see) in perfect working order; yet they do not perform their office of reporting to his brain, because the fluid which animates them is not connected with that brain, but with the brain of the operator.

In a healthy man the spleen does its work in so generous a fashion that the specialized life-force is present in very large quantities, and is constantly radiating from the body in all directions. A man in perfect health, therefore, not only is able to impart some of it to another intentionally, by means of mesmeric passes or otherwise, but is also constantly though unconsciously shedding strength and vitality on those around him. On the other hand, a man who from weakness or other causes is unable to specialize for his own use a sufficient amount of the world's life-force, sometimes, equally unconsciously, acts as a sponge and absorbs the already specialized vitality of any sensitive person who is unfortunate enough to come into contact with him, to his own temporary benefit, no doubt, but often to the serious injury of his victim. Probably most people have experienced this in minor degree, and have found that there is some one among their acquaintances after whose visits they always feel a quite unaccountable weariness and languor; and a similar lassitude is frequently felt by persons who attend spiritualistic séances without taking special precautions against the drain upon their vital force set up in the course of the manifestations.

This radiation produces a striking effect upon the appearance of what we may call the purely physical part of the man's aura. It is well known that tiny particles of dense physical matter are constantly being thrown off from man's body, in insensible perspiration and in other ways; and these particles also are visible to clairvoyant sight as a faint grey mist. These particles are in many cases crystals, and therefore are seen in certain geometrical forms; for example, the tiny cubes of chloride of sodium, or common salt, are among the most frequent. The purely physical part of man's surrounding is sometimes called the health-aura, from the fact that its condition is greatly affected by the health of the body from which it emanates. It is a faint bluish-white, almost colourless, and has the appearance of being striated; that is, it is full of, or perhaps it might rather be said to be composed of, an infinitude of straight lines radiating evenly in all directions from the pores of the body. That at least is the normal condition of these lines when the body is in perfect health; they are separate, orderly, and as nearly parallel as their radiation allows. But on the advent of disease there is an instant change, the lines in the neighbourhood of the part affected becoming erratic, and lying about in all directions in the wildest confusion, or drooping like the stems of faded flowers.

The reason for this curious appearance is itself an interesting one. We find that the rigidity and parallelism of the lines of this health-aura are caused by the constant radiation of life-force from the healthy body; and as soon as this radiation ceases, the lines fall into the confused condition described above. As the patient recovers, the normal radiation of this magnetic

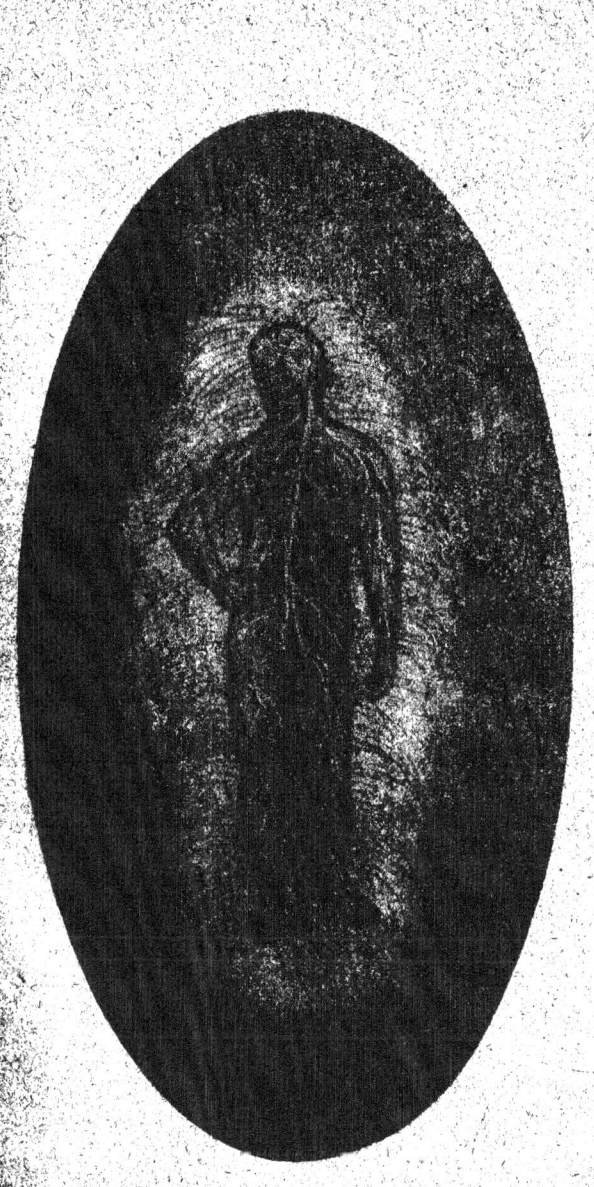

are seen in certain geometrical forms; for example, the tiny cubes of chloride of sodium, or common salt, are among the most frequent. The purely physical part of man's surrounding is sometimes called the health-aura, from the fact that its condition is greatly affected by the health of the body from which it emanates. It is a faint bluish-white, almost colourless, and has the appearance of being striated; that is, it is full of, or perhaps it might rather be said to be composed of, an infinitude of straight lines radiating evenly in all directions from the pores of the body. That at least is the normal condition of these lines when the body is in perfect health; they are quite rigid, orderly, and as nearly parallel as their radiation allows. But on the advent of disease there is an instant change, the lines in the neighbourhood of the part affected becoming erratic, and lying about in all directions in the wildest confusion, or drooping like the stems of faded flowers.

The reason for this curious appearance is itself an interesting one. We find that the rigidity and parallelism of the lines of this health-aura are caused by the constant radiation of life-force from the healthy body; and as soon as this radiation ceases, the lines fall into the confused condition described above. As the patient recovers, the normal radiation of this magnetic

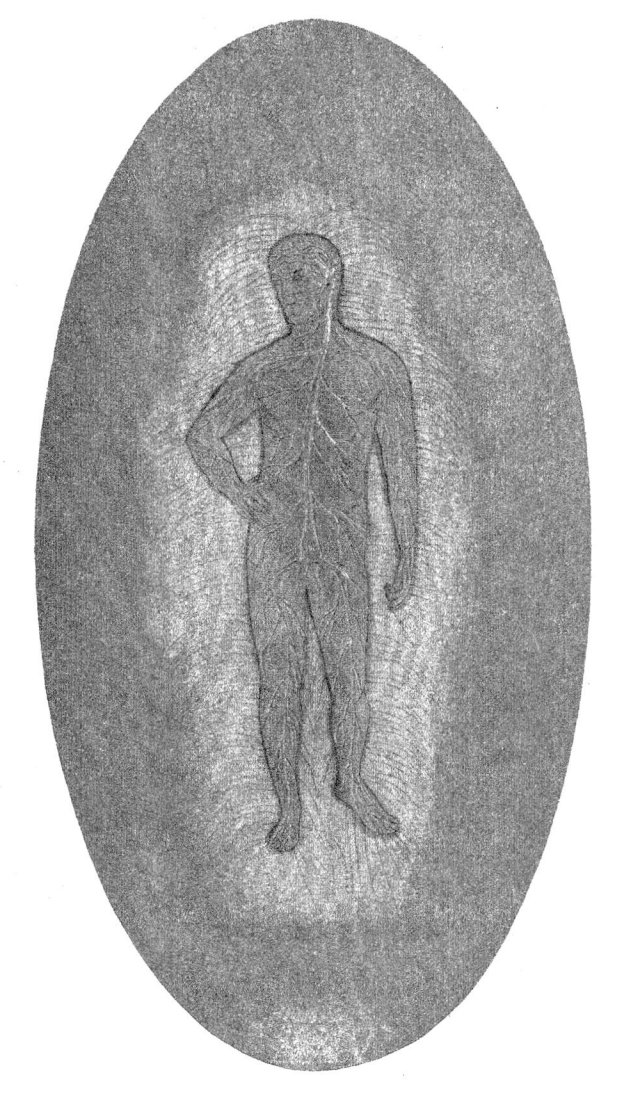

XXV

form of vital energy is gradually resumed, and the lines of the health-aura are thereby combed into order once more. As long as the lines are firm and straight, and the force steadily radiates between them, the body seems to be almost entirely protected from the attack of evil physical influences, such as germs of disease, for example—such germs being repelled and carried away by the out-rush of the life-force; but when from any cause—through weakness, through wound or injury, through over-fatigue, through extreme depression of spirits, or through the excesses of an irregular life—an unusually large amount of vitality is required to repair damage or waste within the body, and there is consequently a serious diminution in the quantity radiated, this system of defence becomes dangerously weak, and it is comparatively easy for the deadly germs to effect an entrance.

It may also be mentioned that it is possible by an effort of will to check this radiation of vitality at the outer extremity of its lines, and there to build it into a kind of wall or shell, which will be absolutely impervious to these germs — and, with a little further effort, impervious also to any kind of astral or elemental influence—so long as such effort of the will is maintained.

Illustrations of this aura, showing its appearance in health and disease respectively, will be found in Plates XXIV. and XXV. It must be remembered that it is almost colourless, so that although it is physical matter, and so needs less developed sight than the astral part of the aura, yet this latter is so much more conspicuous by reason of the brilliancy of its flashing colours and its constant movement, that it is very often seen at an earlier stage of the man's progress than the other.

CHAPTER XX

THE CAUSAL BODY OF THE ADEPT

PROBABLY to those who cannot yet see any of the higher bodies of man, the illustrations given in this book will be to some extent suggestive and even illuminative, and it is in the hope that that may be so that it has been published. Yet those who *can* see, while recognising to the full the painstaking care and skill of the artist, will all agree that even the lowest of these super-physical planes can never be adequately pourtrayed on paper or canvas. If this be true, as it assuredly is, how much more hopelessly impossible (if one may be pardoned the use of an improper, but expressive phrase) must it be to try to represent the Adept—the man who has attained the goal of humanity—who has become something more than man.

In his case the size of the causal body has enormously increased, and shines with a sun-like splendour far beyond all imagination in its glorious loveliness. Of the beauty of form and colour here no words can speak, for mortal language has no terms in which those radiant spheres may be described. Such a vehicle would be a separate study in itself, but one quite beyond the powers of any but those who are already far on the Path.

This at least may be seen, that such a body is not only much larger than that of the ordinary man, but also has its colours differently arranged. These no longer move in whirling clouds, but are arranged in great concentric shells, yet penetrated everywhere by radiations of living light always pouring forth from him as a centre. The order of the colours differs according to the type to which the Adept belongs, so that there are several well-marked varieties amid their glory. Strangely enough, considering the recondite character of the subject, a tradition —a perfectly accurate tradition—of this fact has been preserved in many of the roughly-drawn pictures of the Lord Buddha which one sees upon temple walls in Ceylon. The Great Teacher is usually represented there surrounded by an aura; and the strange thing is that though the colouring and general arrangement of those surroundings would be grotesquely inaccurate and even impossible if intended for that of an ordinary man, or even for that of an ordinary Adept (if one may without irreverence use such an expression), yet it *is* a rough and material representation of the actual higher vehicle of the Adept of that particular type to which this Great One belongs. It is noteworthy also that the lines of the health-aura are drawn in some of these primitive pictures.

If it is impossible to attempt to illustrate the causal body of the Master, it may yet be worth while to give some idea of the relative size and appearance of that of one of His more advanced pupils—one who has attained that fourth stage of the Path which in Oriental books is called that of the Arhat. (See *Invisible Helpers*, p. 119.) Such an endeavour has been made in Plate XXVI., but an effort of the imagination even greater than usual is necessary to complete the picture, by reason of the fact that the colours of this causal body have two characteristics which are irreconcilable here on the physical plane. They are definitely more delicate and etheral than any that have been previously described; yet at the same time they are far fuller, more brilliant and more luminous. Until we can paint with fire instead of mere colour, we shall find ourselves always on one horn or other of the dilemma; for if we attempt to represent the depth and richness of the colour it must look dense and solid; if we try instead to give its marvellous transparency and luminosity, then the colours must be entirely lacking in the wonderful power and brilliancy which is so prominent a characteristic of the glorious reality. Since, however, an effort has been made in the case of the other causal bodies to give an idea of the transparent ovoid form, it seems better in this case to try to give the depth of colour, its arrangement, and the relative size. This last can be brought into proportion only by the expedient of decreasing many times the size of the physical body in our picture; for if we retained the same scale as that previously employed, the causal body of the Arhat would need to be represented as some yards in length and breadth. Consequently we are compelled to reduce very much the drawing of the physical form, in order that the causal body, when drawn in proportion to it, may come within the size of even a double plate. But even at the best, such a drawing can only be regarded as a help to stimulate us in an effort to make a mental image—an image which may perchance be less hopelessly inadequate than the physical representation.

In examining this illustration we are at once struck by the magnificent development of the highest types of intellect, love and devotion, by the wealth of sympathy and of the highest spirituality which it displays. The outrush of the Divine influence which we saw in Plate XXI.

138   MAN VISIBLE AND INVISIBLE

the colours must be entirely wonderful power and brilliancy lacking in the prominent a characteristic of the glorious reality. Since, however, an effort has been made in the case of the other causal bodies to give an idea of the transparent ovoid form, it seems better in this case to try to give the depth of colour, its arrangement, and the relative size. This last can be brought into proportion only by the expedient of decreasing many times the size of the physical body in our picture; for if we retained the same scale as that previously employed, the causal body of the Arhat would need to be represented as some yards in length and breadth. Consequently we are compelled to reduce very much the drawing of the physical form, in order that the causal body, when drawn in proportion to it, may come within the size of even a double plate. But even at the best, such a drawing can only be regarded as a help to stimulate us in an effort to make a mental image—an image which may perchance be less hopelessly inadequate than the physical representation.

In examining this illustration we are at once struck by the magnificent development of the highest types of intellect, love and devotion, by the wealth of sympathy and of the highest spirituality which it displays. The outrush of the Divine influence which we saw in Plate XXI.

XXVI

is enormously intensified here, for this man has become an almost perfect channel for the life and the power of the Logos. Not only in white light does the glory radiate from him, but all the colours of the rainbow play round him in ever changing gleams like mother-of-pearl; so that there is something in that radiation to strengthen the highest qualities in every person who approaches him, no matter what those qualities may be. Thus none can come within the range of his influence without being the better for it; he shines upon all around him like the sun, for, like it, he has become a manifestation of the Logos.

The mind-body and astral body connected with this would have very little characteristic colour of their own, but would be reproductions of the causal body in so far as their lower octaves could express it. They have a lovely shimmering iridescence—a sort of opalescent, mother-of-pearl effect — which is far beyond either description or representation.

One thing at least we may perhaps hope that our study of these inner vehicles will do for us; it may help us to understand that it is this higher presentation of him which is the real man, and not that aggregation of physical matter crystallized in the midst of it, to which we in our blindness attach such undue importance.

The very man himself—the divine trinity within—we may not see; but the more our sight and knowledge increase, the more nearly we approach that which veils Itself in him; and if for the moment the highest vehicle of his which is perceptible to us is the causal body, then that is the nearest to a conception of the true man that our sight will at present give us. But if the same man be looked upon from the standpoint of the lower mental levels, naturally only so much of him can be seen as can be expressed in that mind-body which is the manifestation of the personality. Examining him on the astral plane, we find that an additional veil has descended, and only that lower part of him is visible which can find expression though the vehicle of desire. Here on the physical plane we are still worse off, since the true man is more effectually hidden from us than ever.

Perhaps the knowledge of this may lead us to form a somewhat higher opinion of our fellow-man, since we realise that he is always so much more than he seems to the physical eye. There is always the higher possibility in the background, and often an appeal to the better nature will arouse it from its latency, and bring it down into manifestation where all can see it. When we have studied the man as he is, it may be easier for us to pierce through the dense physical veil, and image the reality which is behind. Our faith in human nature may become greater when we realise how entirely it is part of the divine nature; and so we may be able to help our fellow-man the better, because we grasp the certainty that he and we are one.

If through us the divine light shines out more brightly, it is only in order that we may share that light with him; if we have gained a higher step upon the ladder, it is only that we may stretch out a helping hand to him. The more we understand this glorious scheme of evolution whose progress we have been studying in its outward manifestation, the more fully shall we see the true intention of the mighty self-sacrifice of the Logos; and so beautiful is this, so perfect beyond all thought of ours, that to see it once is to be devoted for ever to its realisation. To see it is to throw oneself into it, to strive for ever more to be one with it, even though in the very humblest capacity; for he who works with God is working for eternity and not for time, and in all the æons that lie before us his work can never fail.

INDEX

ACCESSION of affection, 96
Accession of devotion, 98
Action of irritability, 73
Adept, the, 135
Affection in children, 108
Affinity, chemical, 48
Anger, sudden, 100
Animal consciousness, 49
Animal instincts, 43
Animal intelligence, 61
Animal monad, the, 39
Arhat, the, 137
Aspects of the Logos, 29, 34
Aspirations, spiritual, 120
Astral awakening, 55
Astral body, the, 76, 94
Astral body of savage, 88
Astral impressions, how received, 16
Astral world, the, 10, 22
Astral work, 57
Athanasian Creed, the, 28
Atoms, 9
Aura, the health, 128
Avarice, exhibition of, 110
Average man, the, 92
Awakening upon the astral, 55

BASES of Theosophical knowledge, 3
Bodies of man, the, 13
Buddhi, 22
Building of a shell, 133

CAUSAL body, the, 52, 64, 66, 78, 92, 118
Ceylon, temple pictures in, 136
Characteristics of the Theosophical student, 112, 120
Chemical affinity, 48

Chemistry, occult, 8, 10
Children, affection in, 108
Church, effects seen in, 99
Churches, schism between, 32
Clairvoyance, what it is, 19
Clairvoyant sight, 4, 13
Colours and their meaning, 71, 80, 87, 93, 94
Colours, production of the, 73
Conditions of matter, 7
Consciousness, development of the, 46
Consciousness during sleep, 53
Consciousness, focus of, 16
Consciousness in the animal kingdom, 49
Consciousness, human, 52
Consciousness in the vegetable kingdom, 49
Creed, the Athanasian, 28

DEPRESSION, 111
Descent of the Logos, 31, 36
Desire elemental, the, 39
Developed man, the, 117
Development of consciousness, 46
Devotion, accession of, 98
Devotional type, the, 113
Differentiation, 40, 44
Dimensions, many, 24
Double, the etheric, 128

EFFECT of motion, 73, 96
Effects seen in church, 99
Elemental kingdoms, 38
Elementals, dark and bright, 77
Elementals, desire and mental, 39.
Elements, 8

INDEX

Emotion, effect of, 73, 96
Energy, vital, 129, 132
Equation, the personal, 79
Essence, monadic, 38
Ether, 8
Etheric double, the, 128
Evil, impermanence of, 74
Evolution, moral, 126
Evolution, necessity of, 62
Evolution, Theosophical theory of, 2.
Experiments of Professor Van Schrön, 37

FALLING in love, 105, 107
Fear, 103
Feeling, the process of, 15
First outpouring, 36
Focus of consciousness, 16
Future which awaits us, 126

GRAVITY, specific (of astral matter), 90
Group-soul, the, 40

HEALTH-AURA, the, 128
Holy Ghost, procession of the, 32
How astral impressions are received, 16
Human consciousness, 52

IMPERFECTION of ordinary vision, 19
Impermanence of evil, 74
Impressions (astral), how received, 16
Individualisation, 45
Instincts, animal, 43
Intelligence in the animal, 61
Intense anger, 100
Interpenetration of planes, 11, 12
Irritable man, the, 108
Irritability, action of, 73

JUSTICE, law of, 75

KINGDOMS, elemental, 38

LAW of justice, 75
Life in the mineral, 37
Little worries, 109
Logos, the, 27

Logos, aspect of, 29, 34
Logos, descent into matter of, 31, 36
Love, falling in, 105, 107

MALICE, 100
Man an image of God, 26, 33
Man, the irritable, 108
Man, the real, 139
Man, spiritual, 65
Man, various bodies of, 13
Man's evolution, Theosophical theory of, 2
Many dimensions, 24
Mary, the Virgin, 36
Matter, conditions of, 7
Matter, descent of the Logos into, 31, 36
Meanings of colour, 71, 80, 87, 93, 94
Mechanism of thought, 14
Mental body, 78, 93
Mental elemental, 39
Mental world, 11, 22
Mineral, life in the, 37
Mineral monad, 39
Miser, the, 110
Monadic essence, 38
Monads, mineral and vegetable, 39
Moral evolution, 126

NATURE, planes of, 7
Nimbus, origin of the, 124
Necessity of evolution, 62
Nirvâna, 20

OBSESSION, a man liable to, 101
Occult chemistry, 8, 10
Ordinary man, 92
Origin of the nimbus, 124
Outpouring, the first, 36
Outpouring, the second, 37
Outpouring, the third, 38, 59

PASSION, results of, 102
Past, records of, 30
Person, meaning of, 30
Personal equation, the, 79
Persons of the Logos, 29
Planes, interpenetration of, 11, 12
Planes of Nature, 7, 20, 23
Process of feeling, 15

Procession of the Holy Ghost, 32
Production of the colours, 73
Psychical faculties, how they show themselves, 86

REAL man, the, 139
Reasoning power in animals, 49
Records of the past, 25
Reincarnation, 43, 67
Results of passion, 102
Rush of affection, 96

SALVATION, 126
Savage, the, 87
Savage, astral body of, 88
Schism between churches, 32
Scientific type, the, 114
Second outpouring, 37
Selfishness outgrown, 69
Shell, the building of a, 133
Sight, clairvoyant, 4
Size of the vehicles, 91
Sleep, consciousness during, 53
Souls, younger, 105
Specific gravity of astral matter, 90
Spiritual aspirations, 120
Spiritual man, 65
States of matter, 7
Sudden emotion, effects of, 96
Sympathetic vibration, 74

TEMPLE pictures in Ceylon, 136
Terror, a sudden shock of, 103
Theosophical knowledge, bases of, 3
Theosophical student, characteristics of, 112, 120
Theosophical theory of man's evolution, 2
Third outpouring, the, 38, 59
Thought forms, 125
Thought, mechanism of, 14
Trinity, the, 26
Trishna, 68

VAMPIRES, unconscious, 131
Vegetable consciousness, 49
Vegetable monad, the, 39
Vehicles, relative size of, 91
Vibrations, sympathetic, 74
Virgin Mary, the, 36
Vital energy, 129, 132
Von Schrön, experiments of Professor, 37

WATER spout, illustration of the, 60
What clairvoyance is, 19
Work on the astral, 57
World, the astral, 10
World, the mental, 11, 22
Worries, little, 109

YOUNGER souls, 105

LIST

OF BOOKS RELATING TO

Theosophy, Occultism, Hypnotism, Hermetics, Etc.

Published by

JOHN LANE

THE BODLEY HEAD
67 Fifth Avenue
NEW YORK

BOOKS RELATING TO THEOSOPHY, OCCULTISM, HYPNOTISM, HERMETICS, ETC.

Albertus Magnus. EGYPTIAN SECRETS. Translated from the German. 16mo. $1.00.

Anderson (R. E.). THE STORY OF THE EXTINCT CIVILIZATION OF THE EAST. 16mo. 40 cents.

Arnold (Sir Edwin). THE SONG CELESTIAL; OR, BHAGAVAD GITA. 16mo. Cloth, 75 cents; Leather, $1.00.

Barnes (W. A.). PSYCHOLOGY, HYPNOTISM, PERSONAL MAGNETISM, AND CLAIRVOYANCE. 12mo. Paper, 25c.

Besant (Annie). *ESOTERIC CHRISTIANITY; OR, THE LESSER MYSTERIES. 12mo. $1.50 net.
  THOUGHT POWER. 12mo. 75 cents.
  ANCIENT IDEALS IN MODERN LIFE. 75 cents.
  THE ANCIENT WISDOM. $1.50.
  BHAGAVAD GITA; OR, THE LORD'S SONG. New and Revised Translation. Morocco, $1.00; Leather, 75 cents; Cloth, 50 cents; Paper, 15 cents.
  SOME PROBLEMS OF LIFE. 12mo. 75 cents.
  THE AVATARAS. 12mo. 75 cents.
  THE EVOLUTION OF LIFE AND FORM. 12mo. 75 cents.
  THE STORY OF THE GREAT WAR. 12mo. $1.25. Edition de Luxe, $1.75.
  DHARMA. 12mo. 50 cents.
  AN AUTOBIOGRAPHY. 12mo. $1.75.
  THE BIRTH AND EVOLUTION OF THE SOUL. 12mo. 35c.
  BUILDING OF KOSMOS. 12mo. 75 cents.
  DEATH—AND AFTER? 35 cents.
  ELECTRICITY. Paper, 15 cents.
  FOUR GREAT RELIGIONS. 12mo. 75 cents.
  THE FUTURE THAT AWAITS US. Wrappers, 35 cents.
  IN THE OUTER COURT. 12mo. 75 cents.

Besant (Annie)—*continued.*
KARMA. 35 cents.
LIGHT, HEAT, AND SOUND. 12mo. 75 cents.
MAN AND HIS BODIES. 35 cents.
THE PATH OF DISCIPLESHIP. 12mo. 75 cents.
REINCARNATION. 35 cents.
THE SELF AND ITS SHEATHS. 12mo. 50 cents.
THE SEVEN PRINCIPLES OF MAN. 35 cents.
THE DOCTRINE OF THE HEART. Cloth, 50 cents; Leather, 75 cents.
THE MASTERS AS FACTS AND IDEALS. Paper, 15 cents.
THE PLACE OF PEACE. Paper, 5 cents.
WHY I BECAME A THEOSOPHIST. Paper, 10 cents.
A ROUGH OUTLINE OF THEOSOPHY. Paper, 10 cents.
THE SPHINX OF THEOSOPHY. Paper, 10 cents.
THEOSOPHY IN QUESTIONS AND ANSWERS. Paper, 10c.
THE MEANING AND USE OF PAIN. Paper, 10 cents.
VEGETARIANISM IN THE LIGHT OF THEOSOPHY. Paper, 10c.
THEOSOPHY AND ITS EVIDENCES. Paper, 10 cents.
INTRODUCTION TO THEOSOPHY. Paper, 10 cents.
THEOSOPHY AND CHRISTIANITY. Paper, 5 cents.
IN DEFENSE OF THEOSOPHY. Paper, 8 cents.
EASTERN CASTES AND WESTERN CLASSES. Paper, 10c.
THE PILGRIMAGE OF THE SOUL. Paper, 10 cents.
THE PLACE OF POLITICS IN THE LIFE OF A NATION. Paper, 10 cents.
MATERIALISM UNDERMINED BY SCIENCE. Paper, 10c.
THEOSOPHY AND ITS TEACHINGS. Paper, 10 cents.
1875–1891: A FRAGMENT OF AUTOBIOGRAPHY. Paper, 8c.
THE USE OF EVIL. Paper, 10 cents.
DEVOTION AND THE SPIRITUAL LIFE. Paper, 10 cents.
THEOSOPHY AND THE LAW OF POPULATION. Paper, 5c.
THEOSOPHY AND ITS PRACTICAL APPLICATION. Paper, 3c.

Besant (Annie)—*continued.*
 ON SOME DIFFICULTIES OF THE INNER LIFE. Paper, 10c.
 OCCULTISM, SEMI-OCCULTISM, AND PSEUDO-OCCULTISM. Paper, 15 cents.
 EMOTION, INTELLECT, AND SPIRITUALITY. Paper, 15 cents.
 INDIVIDUALITY. Paper, 15 cents.

*****Besant (Annie)**, A FEW HELPFUL THOUGHTS FROM THE WRITINGS OF. 16mo. 25 cents net.

Bhagavad Gita. *See under* ARNOLD (SIR EDWIN); BESANT (ANNIE); INDIAN LITERATURE; ROW (T. S.).

Blavatsky (H. P.). *ISIS UNVEILED. 2 Vols. Large 8vo. $7.50.
 *THE SECRET DOCTRINE. 2 Vols. and Index. Large 8vo. $12.50 net.
 *THE SECRET DOCTRINE. Vol. III. Large 8vo. $5.00 net.
 *INDEX TO THE SECRET DOCTRINE. Contains a Key adapting it to the old editions. Large 8vo. $5.00 net.
 *KEY TO THEOSOPHY. 8vo. $2.00 net.
 *A MODERN PANARION: a Collection of Fugitive Fragments. 8vo. $2.50 net.
 *GEMS FROM THE EAST. 12mo. Leather, 75 cents net.
 *NIGHTMARE TALES. 12mo. Paper, 35 cents net.
 *THE VOICE OF THE SILENCE. Leather, 75 cents net; Cloth, 50 cents.

Blavatsky (H. P.) and Collins (Mabel). *FIRST STEPS IN OCCULTISM. 16mo. 50 cents net.

Bowden (E. M.). *THE IMITATION OF BUDDHA. 16mo. $1.00 net.

Brodbeck (Adolf). THE IDEAL OF UNIVERSITIES. 12mo. $1.50.

Brodie-Innes (J. W.). THE TRUE CHURCH OF CHRIST—EXOTERIC AND ESOTERIC. 12mo. $1.25.

Burgoyne (T. H.). *THE LIGHT OF EGYPT. 8vo. Vol. I. Paper, $1.00 net; Cloth, $2.00 net; Vol. II. Cloth only, $2.00 net.

*CELESTIAL DYNAMICS. 12mo. $1.00 net.

*THE LANGUAGE OF THE STARS. Paper, 50 cents net.

Caird (Mona). *THE MORALITY OF MARRIAGE. 12mo. $2.25 net.

Caithness (Countess of). *A MIDNIGHT VISIT TO HOLYROOD. 12mo. $1.75 net.

Carus (Paul). THE GOSPEL OF BUDDHA. 12mo. Paper, 35 cents; Cloth, $1.00.

Cassecanarie (S. M. D.). *OBEAH SIMPLIFIED: THE TRUE WANGA. 8vo. Paper, 35 cents net.

*Collectanea Chemica: Being Select Treatises on Alchemy, etc., by Eirenæus Philatethes, Sir George Ripley, and others. 12mo. $2.50 net.

*Collectanea Hermetica. Edited by W. Wynn Westcott, M. B.

Vol. I. HERMETIC ARCANUM OF PENES NOS UNDA TAGI 1623. 12mo. $1.00 net.
Vol. II. THE PYMANDER OF HERMES. 12mo. $1.25 net.
Vol. III. A SHORT ENQUIRY CONCERNING THE HERMETIC ART. 12mo. $1.00 net.
Vol. IV. ÆSCH MEZAREPH; OR, PURIFYING FIRE. 12mo. $1.00 net.
Vol. V. SOMNIUM SCIPIONIS AND THE GOLDEN VERSES OF PYTHAGORAS. 12mo. $1.00 net.
Vol. VI. THE CHALDEAN ORACLES OF ZOROASTER. 12mo. $1.00 net.
Vol. VII. EUPHRATES; OR, THE WATERS OF THE EAST. 12mo. $1.25 net.
Vol. VIII. EGYPTIAN MAGIC. 12mo. $1.50 net.

Collins (Mabel). *THE BLOSSOM AND THE FRUIT. 12mo. $1.50 net.

*IDYLL OF THE WHITE LOTUS. 12mo. $1.50 net.

*LIGHT ON THE PATH. Morocco, $1.00 net; Leather, 75 cents net; Cloth, 40 cents net; Paper, 25 cents net.

Collins (Mabel)—*continued.*
   *The Story of the Year. 16mo. 50 cents net.
   *Through the Gates of Gold. 12mo. 50 cents net.
      See also Blavatsky (H. P.).

Cooper-Oakley (Mrs.). *Traces of a Hidden Tradition in Masonry and Mediæval Mysticism. 12mo. $1.25 net.

Cotton (Louise). *Palmistry and its practical Uses. 12mo. $1.00 net.

Dale (Mrs.). *Indian Palmistry. 12mo. 35 cents net.

Das Bhagavan (M. A.). *The Science of the Emotions. 12mo. $1.25 net.

Davids (Prof. T. W. Rhys). *Buddhism, its History and Literature. 12mo. $1.50 net.

Dowd (F. B.). Double Man: a Novel. 12mo. Paper, 50 cents; Cloth, $1.00.
   The Temple of the Rosy Cross. 12mo. $1.25.

Du Prel (Baron). *Philosophy of Mysticism. Translated by C. C. Massey. 2 vols. 8vo. $7.50 net.

Duff (R.). *Civilization of India. 16mo. 50 cents net.

Dvivedi (Prof. M. N.). *The Initiation of S'ankara. 12mo. $1.60 net.
   *The Mandukyopanishad. 12mo. $1.50 net.
   *Monism or Advaitism? 12mo. Paper, 50 cents net.
   *Yoga-sutra. 12mo. $1.00 net.

Edger (Lilian). *Theosophy Applied. 12mo. 75 cents net.

*Egyptian Magic. By S.S.D.D. 12mo. $1.50 net.

Ellis (Ida). *A Catechism of Palmistry. 12mo. $1.00 net.

Goodrich-Freer (A.). Essays in Psychical Research. 12mo. $2.50.
   The Alleged Haunting of B— House. 12mo. $1.25.

H. A. V. *THE MYSTIC GUIDE IN THE GOSPEL ACCORDING TO ST. JOHN. 12mo. 50 cents net.

Hargrove (E. T.). *LIFE'S QUESTIONS. 12mo. $1.00 net.
*SOME MODERN FAILINGS. 12mo. Paper, 10 cents net.

Harrison (E. G.). *THE TRANSCENDENTAL UNIVERSE. Six lectures on Occult Science and Theosophy. 12mo. $1.00 net.

Hartmann (Franz). *PARACELSUS. 12mo. $1.50 net.
*MAGIC, WHITE AND BLACK. 8vo. $2.50 net.
*IN THE PRONAOS OF THE TEMPLE OF WISDOM. 8vo. $2.50 net.
*JEHOSHUA. 12mo. $1.50 net.
*OCCULT SCIENCE IN MEDICINE. 12mo. $1.25 net.
*TALKING IMAGE OF URUR. 12mo. $1.50 net.
*AMONG THE GNOMES. 12mo. Paper, 75 cents net; Cloth, $1.75 net.
*AN ADVENTURE AMONG THE ROSICRUCIANS. 12mo. 75 cents net.
*THE CORRELATION OF SPIRITUAL FORCES. 12mo. Paper, 40 cents net.
*BURIED ALIVE. 12mo. Paper, 35 cents net; Cloth, 75 cents net.

Heidenhain (Rudolph). *HYPNOTISM. 12mo. $1.00 net.

***Hermetic Museum, The.** Restored and enlarged. Now first done into English. Edited by A. E. Waite. In 2 vols. Small 4to. $14.00 net.

Hinton (C. H.). *SCIENTIFIC ROMANCES. First and second series. 12mo. $2.00 net, each.
NEW ERA OF THOUGHT. 12mo. $2.00 net.

H. P. B. In Memory of Helena Petrovina Blavatsky. By some of Her pupils. Wrappers. Sq. 8vo. 35 cents.

***Iamblichus.** Trans. by Thomas Taylor. Sq. 8vo. $2.50 net.

*Indian Literature, Society for the Resuscitation of.
18mo. 50 cents net per vol.
THE VEDAS—THE DARSHANA—THE PURANAS—SANKARACHARYA—
THE UPANISHADS—BHAGAVAT-GITA—DRAMAS—AYURVEDA.

Isavasyopanishad, The. Translated into English by S. Chandra Vasa. Boards. 8vo. 50 cents.

Jennings (Hargrave). *THE INDIAN RELIGIONS. 8vo. $3.50 net.

Kingsford (Anna). *ASTROLOGY THEOLOGIZED. Illustrated. 8vo. $3.00 net.

*THE PERFECT WAY. 8vo. $2.50 net.

*THE VIRGIN OF THE WORLD. 8vo. $4.00 net.

*THE PERFECT WAY IN DIET. 12mo. 75 cents net.

Kingsland (W.). *ESOTERIC BASIS OF CHRISTIANITY. 12mo. $1.75 net.

*MYSTIC QUEST: A TALE OF TWO INCARNATIONS. 12mo. $1.75 net.

Leadbeater (C. W.). ASTRAL PLANE. 35 cents.

THE AURA. Paper, 5 cents.

CHRISTIAN CREED. 12mo. 50 cents.

CLAIRVOYANCE. 12mo. 75 cents.

DEVACHANIC PLANE. 35 cents.

DREAMS. 12mo. 50 cents.

INVISIBLE HELPERS. 12mo. 50 cents.

NEW CHARTER; a Discussion of the Rights of Men and the Rights of Animals. 75 cents.

OUR RELATION TO CHILDREN. Paper, 15 cents.

Levi (Eliphas). *MAGICAL RITUAL OF THE SANCTUM REGNUM. 12mo. $2.50 net.

*TRANSCENDENTAL MAGIC. 8vo. $6.00 net.

Massey (Gerald). *A BOOK OF THE BEGINNINGS. 2 vols. Large 8vo. $6.00 net.

*THE NATURAL GENESIS. 2 vols. Large 8vo. $6.00 net.

Mathers (S. L. M.). *THE KABBALAH UNVEILED. 8vo. $3.50 net.
*THE KEY OF SOLOMON THE KING. 8vo. $8.00 net.

Mead (G. A. S.). THE GOSPELS AND THE GOSPEL. 12mo. $1.50.
APOLLONIUS OF TYANA: THE PHILOSOPHER-REFORMER OF THE FIRST CENTURY, A. D. A Critical Study. 8vo. $1.25.
*FRAGMENTS OF A FAITH FORGOTTEN: a Contribution to the Study of Christian Origins. 8vo. $2.50 net.
*PISTIS SOPHIA: a Gnostic Gospel. 8vo. $2.50 net.
*ORPHEUS. 12mo. $1.50 net.
*PLOTINUS. 12mo. 35 cents net.
*SIMON MAGUS: an Essay. Large 8vo. Boards. $1.75 net.
*THE WORLD MYSTERY. 12mo. $1.75 net.

Nizida. *THE ASTRAL LIGHT: an Attempted Exposition of Certain Occult Principles in Nature. 12mo. 85 cents net.

Olcott (H. S.). *OLD DIARY LEAVES. First and second series. 12mo. $2.00 net each.
*POSTHUMOUS HUMANITY. 12mo. $2.50 net.
*THEOSOPHY, RELIGION, AND OCCULT SCIENCE. 12mo. $2.50 net.

Old (W. Gorn) [Sepharial]. *NEW MANUAL OF ASTROLOGY. 8vo. $4.00 net.

Oman (J. C.). *THE GREAT INDIAN EPICS. 12mo. $1.50 net.

Orpheus, The Mystical Hymns of. *See under* TAYLOR (THOMAS).

Owen (John). *EVENINGS WITH THE SKEPTICS. 2 vols. 8vo. $4.50 net.

Owen (R. Dale). *Footprints on the Boundary of Another World. 8vo. $3.00 net.
*Debatable Land Between This World and the Next. 8vo. $3.00 net.
*Threading My Way. 8vo. $3.00 net.

Papus. *See* Tarot of the Bohemians.

*Paracelsus, The Hermetic and Alchemical Writing of. For the first time faithfully translated into English. 2 vols. 8vo. $18.00 net.

Pilgrim. *The Great Secret. 12mo. $2.50 net.
*A Blank Page. 12mo. $2.00 net.

Plotinus. *See under* Taylor (Thomas).

Pope (Mary). *Novel Dishes for Vegetarian Households. 12mo. $1.25.

Porphyry. *The Philosopher to His Wife Marcella. 12mo. $1.25 net.

*Prabodha Chandrodaya; or, Rise of the Moon of Intellect. Translated by J. Taylor. 8vo. Boards. 65 cents net.

Prasad (Rama). *Essays on Nature's Finer Forces.
The Science of Breath, and the Philosophy of the Tattvas. 12mo. $1.50 net.

Rosenroth (Knorr Von). Æsch Mezareph. *See under* Collectanea Hermetica.

Row (T. Subha). *Collection of Esoteric Writings. 8vo. Boards. $1.75 net.
*Lectures on the Study of the Bhagavad Gita. 12mo. Boards. 75 cents net.

Scott-Elliott (W.). The Marriage of the Soul, and Other Poems. 85 cents.
The Story of Atlantis. $1.25.

Sepher Yetzirah. *The Book of Formation. Translated from the Hebrew by W. W. Westcott. 12mo. $1.00 net.

Sinnett (A. P.). Nature's Mysteries. 12mo. 75 cents.
  *Esoteric Buddhism. 12mo. $1.25 net.
  *The Growth of the Soul as Illuminated by Esoteric Teachings. 12mo. $1.50 net.
  *The Occult World. 12mo. $1.25 net.
  *Karma: a Novel. 12mo. 75 cents net.
  *Appolonius of Tyana. 12mo. Paper, 35 cents net.
  *The Constitution of the Ego. 12mo. Paper, 35 cts. net.
  *The Beginnings of the Fifth Race. 12mo. Paper, 35 cents net.
  *The Human Aura. 12mo. Paper, 35 cents net.
  *Karma. 12mo. Paper, 35 cents net.
  *Modern Spiritualism. 12mo. Paper, 35 cents net.
  *The Path of Initiation. 12mo. Paper, 35 cents net.
  *The System to Which we Belong. 12mo. 35 cents net.

*****Spirit's Idea of Happiness, The.** Edited by J. R. Tutin. 12mo. $1.00 net.

Stead (W. T.). Letters from Julia; or, Light from the Borderland. 75 cents.

*****Tarot of the Bohemians, The.** The most ancient book in the world. By Papus. Translated by A. P. Morton. 12mo. $2.25 net.

Tatya (Tukaran). *Guide to Theosophy. 8vo. Boards. $1.60 net.

Taylor (Thomas). *The Mystical Hymns of Orpheus. Translated. 12mo. $1.75 net.
  *Select Works of Plotinus. Translated into English. 12mo. $1.60 net.
        See also Iamblichus.

Temple (Ernest). *Life's Questions. 12mo. $1.00 net.

*****Theosophist, The.** Conducted by Colonel Olcott. Annual subscription, $5.00 net; single copies, 50 cents net.

Theosophy, Five Years of. 8vo. $3.25 net.

Tutin (J. R.). *See* SPIRIT'S IDEA OF HAPPINESS.

Tyner (Paul). THE LIVING CHRIST. 12mo. $1.00.
THROUGH THE INVISIBLE. 12mo. 75 cents.

*Upanishads, The Theosophy of. PART I. SELF AND NOT SELF. 12mo. $1.00 net.

*Vasudevamanana: or, the Meditations of Vasudeva. Translated from the Sanskrit by K. N. Aierano, R. S. Sastri. 12mo. Paper, 50 cents net.

Vaughan (R. A.). *HOURS WITH THE MYSTICS. 2 vols. 12mo. $2.50 net.

Vaughan (Thomas). *MAGICAL WRITINGS. 12mo. $3.00 net.

EUPHRATES. *See under* COLLECTANEA HERMETICA.

Vijnana Bhikshu. *THE YOGASARA-SANGRAHA. Translated by Gangânâtha Jha. 12mo. Boards. 75 cts. net.

Vincent (R. H.). *THE ELEMENTS OF HYPNOTISM. 12mo. $1.75 net.

Von Eckartshausen. *THE CLOUD UPON THE SANCTUARY. 12mo. $1.50 net.

Waite (A. S.). *THE BOOK OF BLACK MAGIC AND PACTS. 8vo. $14.00 net.

*LIVES OF ALCHEMYSTICAL PHILOSOPHERS. 8vo. $3.00 net.

*THE OCCULT SCIENCES. 12mo. $2.00 net.

*DEVIL WORSHIP IN FRANCE. 12mo. $2.00 net.

*THE REAL HISTORY OF THE ROSICRUCIANS. 12mo. $2.00 net.

*MYSTERIES OF MAGIC. 8vo. $3.00 net.

*AZOTH. 12mo. $1.75 net.

*THE GOLDEN STAIRS. 12mo. 85 cents net.

*TURBA PHILOSOPHORUM; OR, ASSEMBLY OF THE SAGES. 12mo. $2.50 net.

See also LEVI (ELIPHAS); VAUGHAN (T.); and HERMETIC MUSEUM.

ESOTERIC CHRISTIANITY
By ANNIE BESANT

12mo. $1.50 net

The Opinions of some Leading Authorities

Charles Gordon Ames: "I have gone through Mrs. Besant's book with deep and continuous interest. . . It impresses me as a valuable contribution to a better understanding of both Theosophy and Christianity."

Frederic Willard Parke: "It must be emphatically affirmed of this work, that the thesis which its author proposes to defend is demonstrated with intelligible and convincing proofs. . . A help not often proffered to the devout soul."

Lilian Whiting: "A remarkable book. . . Very subtle and firm in its philosophy. . . It has the large grasp of all contemporary thought; the deep knowledge of Oriental wisdom and of all the philosophies; the sincere, reverent spirit and that crystal clearness of expression that characterizes Annie Besant. . . It may well be described as an epoch-making book."

Rev. John Eills: "It reflects the fact. . . Mrs. Besant writes as one, not at the circumference, but very near the centre of life. . . She vibrates and radiates, or speaks a living word."

N. Y. Tribune: "All who believe there is an esoteric element in Christianity will read this book with delight. The sincerity of the author, her wide range of learning, and the high spiritual uplift of her words, give a high value to her book."

Philadelphia Press: "She voices a great and widespread passion."

Detroit Free Press: "She voices the crying heart and soul needs of those whom church and doctrine have never satisfied . . the new significance of the whole teaching of Jesus. One cannot lay down the book without a sense of both spiritual and intellectual satisfaction."

Louisville Evening Post: "Of great and intrinsic interest. Of its earnest faith and reverent spirit there can be no manner of doubt."

The International Studio
An Illustrated Magazine of Fine and Applied Art

Published by JOHN LANE
The Bodley Head
67 Fifth Avenue, New York City

35 cents per Month. Annual Supscription, $3.50
Three Months' Trial Subscription, $1.00
Two Specimen Copies sent, post free, for 25 cents

IT is the aim of "The International Studio" to treat of every Art and Craft—Architecture, Sculpture, Painting, Ceramics, Metal, Glass, Furniture, Decoration, Design, Bookbinding, Illustrating, Photography, Lithography, Enamel, Jewelry, Needlework, Gardening, etc. The principal writers on Art are contributors to its pages. Many original illustrations, reproduced in every variety of black and white process, half-tone, line, photogravure, etc., are to be found in each number. Color plates of real value are to be found in every issue. No magazine can boast a more artistic and sumptuous get-up than "The International Studio."

Everyone interested in Art, professionally or otherwise, should read it; for the magazine keeps its readers *au fait* with the doings of the art world, both literary and technical.

CPSIA information can be obtained
at www.ICGtesting.com
Printed in the USA
LVOW13s2221010718
582454LV00043B/308/P